SOLO
DAD
SURVIVAL
GUIDE

SOLO DAD SURVIVAL GUIDE

RAISING YOUR KIDS ON YOUR OWN

Reginald F. Davis
Nicholas F. Borns

CB

CONTEMPORARY BOOKS

Library of Congress Cataloging-in-Publication Data

Davis, Reginald F.
    Solo dad survival guide : raising your kids on your own /
    Reginald F. Davis and Nicholas F. Borns.
        p.   cm.
    ISBN 0-8092-2925-0
    1. Single fathers.   2. Child rearing.   3. Father and child.
I. Borns, Nicholas F.   II. Title.
HQ759.915.D38   1998
306.85′6—dc21   98-26011
                                        CIP

Cover design by Scott Rattray
Cover illustration copyright © Mona Daly/Artville, LLC.
Interior design by Scott Rattray

Published by Contemporary Books
An imprint of NTC/Contemporary Publishing Company, Inc.
4255 West Touhy Avenue, Lincolnwood (Chicago), Illinois 60646-1975 U.S.A.

Printed in the United States of America.
International Standard Book Number: 0-8092-2925-0
99 00 01 02 03 04 QP 18 17 16 15 14 13 12 11 10 9 8 7 6 5 4 3 2 1

To Karl Ludwig, Nicholas Kurt, and Christina Colleen Borns

and

Michael Evan, Andrea Elizabeth, and Paul Edward Davis.

Without you, we would never have the chance to be solo dads.

And in memory of Ilsa Anna and Stephen Eric Borns.

Contents

Acknowledgments ix

Introduction: The Brotherhood of Solo Dad xi

Part I: Taking Care of the Kids 1

1. First Things First: Get Ready 3

2. Care and Feeding 17

3. Help! 41

4. My Life as Solo Dad: Nick's Story 55

Part II: Taking Care of Mom 69

5. The Case of the Missing Mom 71

6. My Life as Solo Dad: Reg's Story 81

Part III: Taking Care of Yourself 91

7. Last Things First: Your Emotional Health 93

8. Fathers of the World, Unite! 107

Acknowledgments

THIS BOOK IS REALLY the result of two friends, who share the experience of being single fathers, pooling their life experiences to help each other and, we hope, others in our situation. Therefore, the first acknowledgment should be to those who taught us how to succeed in this experience—our parents. So, to Marje Borns and the late Walter Borns, and to the late Harold and Frances Davis Ford, two sons' deepest appreciation for the examples they gave and for completing a task we now know is the hardest and most rewarding of all.

Friends, family, and supervisors and co-workers have played essential roles in helping us through these child-rearing years, and our thanks go to all of them. Nick would like to thank his sister, Claire Ellsworth; and Reg, his sister, Danielle Wilkinson, for their assistance, advice, and especially their patience in listening to two little brothers complain about their problems and fears. Reg would also like to thank Lillie Hoskins Stiggers, a friend whose help was invaluable in some of the roughest years. And he wishes to cite two top bosses at the *Chicago Tribune*. Managing Editor Ann Marie Lipinski and Editor Howard Tyner provided not only understanding; their encouragement led directly to the formulation and publication of this book.

Introduction:
The Brotherhood of Solo Dad

Or How to Wallpaper Eighteen
Rooms Using Step-by-Step Audio
Instructions Broadcast in
Bulgarian Through a Tin Can
and String While Trying to Feed
Colicky Goldfish

So, HOW DO you know you have become a solo dad?

Don't laugh; it's not so easy. Even the two of us, former college roommates with twenty-five years of friendship, didn't recognize our bonding in the brotherhood of single fathers for quite some time. Others we have met haven't realized it yet, though we all share the same challenges and rewards.

For some of us it's quick. A door slams, a phone rings, and whatever words are said, the message is clear: the mother of your children is gone.

But for others the transition is not so clear cut. A brief illness becomes an extended recuperation, or a business trip turns into a project assignment. The fluid state of the American family may create any number of situations where a man becomes primary caregiver for one child or several.

The truth is, you don't have to be the permanent, sole caregiver to reach solo dad status. A man can transform into solo dad for several hours one night a week, on regular weekends, for two months a year, or for the rest of his life—but more about this later.

Each of us reached our current state of solo dad in a different way. For Reg, it was that closing door:

RD: As my failing marriage finally imploded (during the last trip to the marriage counselor) in 1993, we had to make some decisions quickly. Her initial desire was to leave, to have some time to herself. There was still a month left for school, and at one point she talked about taking our preschooler to her mother's house while I kept the other two. I was not keen on that idea, but I was solid on one thing— I wanted to play a major role in my kids' lives, no matter where their parents lived.

She changed her mind about separating the kids before she ever left. After that there was some jockeying, some discussion, some fighting—mostly through the lawyers. We finally brokered a settlement that allowed the kids and me to stay in our current home while she pursued her education and kept a residence where she could see them at least one day a week.

I don't want to get too deep into details—payments, visitation, responsibilities. My ex-wife and I get along; we cooperate on the kids and even gossip now and again. But there is one thing she never told me, though other people have said she told them, that might explain how we wound up this way: she knew I would do a good job raising the kids; she was not worried about that.

But I was worried, especially that first full day that she was gone. It was like waking up on the beach and seeing a wave swiftly rising a hundred feet above me. Suddenly all the tasks I hadn't thought about, all the activities that each took a little bit of time, all the responsibilities that I had thought were shared became mine. Just mine. Three pairs of eyes were on me, expecting me not only to bring home the paycheck but to buy the food and get it cooked too, get them to bed and up and off to school, heal wounds and speak in tongues—at least the language of homework. I really worried then.

But I soon found out that worrying has nothing to do with it. Getting things done has everything to do with it. Now I'm usually too busy to worry until it's 2:00 A.M. and whatever the problem was, it's all over by then.

Nick's transformation was quite different:

NB: There are some cases where it's not quite so obvious that you're actually becoming a single parent. And that was what I went through, because I wasn't really aware that I had to keep taking over more and more of the responsibilities.

I was the one who was supposed to go to sea, and Mom was supposed to be there and run all this stuff. Then I would come back and we'd have fun, and then I'd go back to sea again.

But it worked out to be exactly the opposite. She went to the hospital for a week, a couple of weeks, a couple of months, and it just kind of sneaked in on me till I stopped to think, "How long have I been doing this?" That's why I can say, "Well, I've been a single parent for fifteen years," even though I've been divorced for only about seven.

My wife was going into hospitals for psychiatric care for longer and longer periods of time. The cycle was that she would go into the hospital for intensive care, then the hospital would say, "OK, she can be released now." But I just didn't believe she could come right back into the family situation and handle everything. She needed some kind of transition period, a halfway house or something.

And we tried some of that, but every time we did, it was stopped by either the doctors, the hospital, or her relatives, who were the nearest relatives we had.

It was around 1988. I had gotten out of the navy, and it reached a point where I was faced with a decision, and child welfare agencies became involved. At this point we were still married legally, though she was living with her parents, getting treatment. She came down to the house in Madison, Indiana, and a caseworker talked to her. Then the caseworker called me on the phone at work and said, "Is she staying or not? If she's staying, then we're going to have to do something with the kids."

So I was given a choice by the caseworker right there: (*a*) I could handle a full-time job, a part-time job, and all of the stuff at home and the kids, or (*b*) I could take care of my wife. I chose (*a*).

Choosing or being forced to choose, slow transition or sudden change, more and more men are becoming solo dads.

United States census figures from 1992 show that 1.4 million American households, with roughly 2 million minor children, are headed by a single father. An additional 2 million men are stay-at-home fathers, serving as the primary, but in most cases not the sole, caregiver.

The reasons for this growth are almost as numerous as the number of families affected. Many of the reasons are tied to the economic and social sea change that has made us a nation of two-income families. As women assert their rights to their own lives and livelihoods, it becomes more possible, more likely, more necessary that men participate in parenting. As business and industry downsize, reengineer, diversify, and outsource, the traditional family (which was never all that traditional) has been forced to retool and reorganize itself.

But one of the most important reasons that we can see is the rising desire for men to play a bigger role in the rearing of their children. Being a father today means more than being a walking paycheck, a father-daughter dance partner, and a pitching machine in the occasional game of catch. Now, whether it is due to the Iron John men's movement, concern about juvenile crime, or the Promise Keepers and political-religious debates about a man's role, more men are choosing to have deeper and broader relationships with their kids.

We like to believe it is because we men have found that involved fatherhood is fulfilling, deeply satisfying, and comforting to our souls. It also gives us more time to act like kids, and what could be more masculine than that?

With more fathers playing bigger roles, more fathers are becoming solo dads, at least part-time or temporarily. In fact, it's getting hard to find any of us who aren't solo dads at least some of the time.

So, now that you know that you, too, may be a solo dad, how do you do it?

Unfortunately, there haven't been many good books written on this subject. And believe us, we've looked. Look for a fatherhood section in your bookstore or library, and you'll get the first indication—there is no fatherhood section. OK, so fatherhood is parenting, and the parenting section has plenty of titles with *father* in them. Some of them even look at the father's role, methods, and manner as something different from those of the mother, which they most definitely are.

Many are written by psychologists and social scientists, students of family life. Reading their books, you wonder if any of them ever had a family life. Piaget wrote some good things to know, but does he teach us anything about buying pants a five-year-old can snap (and especially unsnap) in the kindergarten bathroom? Scientific sorting-out often doesn't put things in context, especially not the complex context of family interaction.

Of course, we all could take the manly route and do it without advice—fall back on what our lives with our own fathers were like. Except that what got a lot of us men wanting to be more involved with our kids is that our fathers were not involved with us. For many baby boomers, having a dad who changed your diapers was a rarity. It was Paycheck Dad, Pitcher Dad, You-Can't-Have-The-Car-Tonight Dad. And the dads who came after, in the sixties and seventies, may have had more desire but just as little know-how.

Support groups for fathers are nearly impossible to find. Most of those that do exist treat fatherhood as a social problem, a dysfunction that complicates poverty, unemployment, and youth crime. Single fathers themselves are often isolated. Meanwhile, single mothers' groups can too often turn into daddy shopping (or mommy shopping), or so much sympathy and support is offered that the guy feels babied himself.

And that is where we come in. Together, we have over twenty years of child-rearing experience. We may not be up on the latest psychological theory, but we've had hundreds of evenings of figuring out menus and dozens of mornings with last-minute homework. Our experience is practical and hands-on, and we preach only what we have practiced.

Neither of us will claim to be a super-dad, with perfect children and soaring careers and better homes and gardens. We are just here to share what we've learned with all the solo dads who feel truly alone against the minihorde, and even those part-time soloists who need to hear a few encouraging words. It is our intention to be as open and helpful as possible, to talk about what we know and what we have learned, especially from each other, and to be inclusive of all males who would nurture their offspring under whatever circumstances they face.

Our intent is to use a question-and-answer format to make it easier for the reader to find information about one particular situation.

All together, we hope to transmit the message that fathering is fun, fulfilling, and, on rare occasion, easy. Well, as easy as wallpapering eighteen rooms using step-by-step audio instructions broadcast in Bulgarian through a tin can and string while trying to feed colicky goldfish.

Part I

Taking Care of the Kids

THIS IS WHERE you start, with one or three or even more sets of young eyes looking at you hungrily. So, do you just go out for burgers?

Watching your youngsters for any time longer than it takes Mom to buy shoes requires more than a drive-up window. What do you do first? How do you do that, and that, and that, too? And why don't they appreciate it?

We've tried to hit the significant points of taking care of your kids under three chapter headings:

Chapter 1—First Things First: Get Ready. Here we talk about priorities and mind-set, because getting yourself ready and getting yourself into it can take much more time than necessary if you let insecurity stand in the way.

Chapter 2—Care and Feeding. The nuts and bolts of child rearing include food, standards and limits, discipline, shopping and housekeeping, entertainment, and education. This chapter separates the nuts and the bolts and sizes them for your lifestyle.

Chapter 3—Help! Sometimes you need to hire help from outside, and sometimes you need to ask for the assistance of those already inside your life, including your boss, your ex, and even, heaven forbid, your kids.

But those eyes aren't getting any less hungry. Let's get started!

First Things First: Get Ready

SHORT TERM OR LONG, becoming a solo dad takes some getting used to. Most often there is little time to get used to it, but that is not a contradiction, just a complication.

You may walk in the door from work, and your wife hands you a baby, says, "I have got to go," and walks out. She doesn't have to be gone forever—just an hour or two. You may already be prepared—the bottles of formula are in the fridge, the diaper is fresh, bathwater is running, a schedule is outlined in your mind or outlined in red on the kid's bedroom door. Or nothing may have been prepared and you are clueless (a common state for dads). These details make no difference, because if you haven't prepared yourself mentally, no schedule, stocked fridge, or diaper bag in the world will help.

Just two hours with a cranky two-month-old can bring a good day to a screeching halt. And if you spend those two hours waiting for Mom to come home to deal with it, you are cheating both yourself and your child. Learning to deal with the problems of parenting is a big part of the fun of parenting. Just like everything else, doing the thing and learning how to do it is much more fun than waiting for somebody else to do it (except for cleaning bathrooms).

Perhaps the most important point we can make in this book is that every man has got to find his own balance in parenting. He has got to find his own way to get things done and to get his love expressed to his kids. It has to be his way and not just a copy of Mom's way, or it won't work for him or the children.

The solo dad among us who had those evenings with a cranky daughter found that bottles and pacifiers did not work, because she would not let her quivering little lips touch rubber nipples. Holding didn't work; bouncing didn't work; baby swings didn't work; and "Lay her down and let her cry" certainly didn't work. Finally, fearing he might never develop a relationship with Daddy's Little Girl, he got up and walked— and she stopped crying. Mom wasn't happy with all the walking; she was afraid to have her daughter "spoiled" and her times with baby turned into mile-long strolls. But that didn't happen (mainly because a breast-feeding mom has an advantage that a dad just can't match). Instead, the dad and daughter got a chance to bond in their own way as the baby outgrew her crying and Dad outgrew his fear.

We want to relate to all fathers how each of us got past the fear to the fun of being a solo dad.

RD: I remember specifically the moment that I realized I was a single father, the same week that my wife moved out. My two oldest, Michael and Andrea, were in school, and I had taken that Friday off from work. I had used up the time I had for tears, and so I was out at lunch with my youngest, Paul, the preschool dropout. The restaurant

was a hot dog stand near the local high school, but in the early afternoon there wasn't much of a crowd. I gave Paul his chocolate milk,
then peeled the paper wrapping off his hot dog and wrapped it in a
napkin. All of this I had learned from his mother as the way to get
him to eat.

Well, I finished preparations and looked up to hand him the sand-
wich and, at the same time, he put down an empty milk carton and
announced, "Not hungry, Daddy." (The child still lives on air as his
main food group.)

I felt lost—stupid, unprepared, vulnerable, and lost. How could I
forget that kids eat easy, not as we'd like them to? I had even been
told about Paul's proclivity toward filling up on liquids.

Suddenly my mind raced ahead. In a few hours I would need to
pick up the other two from school. And there was dinner; I hadn't
thought about dinner. And there were clothes at the dry cleaner to
pick up. Groceries to buy. Gas for the car? Did I need to do laundry?
Did I read the paper, as all newspaper editors should each day? What
about homework? Baths? Bedtime?

The tasks piled up like scandals at the White House. What do I
do, and what first, and what to finish and, and, and . . . ?

What pulled me out of panic mode, as Paul calmly slid under the
table to play on the floor, was the voice of my late mother. From that
back-corner recess where I stored all those memories of "You know
you should have," "Why didn't you think," and the occasional "You did
great, but that's what you are supposed to do," I heard dear old Mom
say: "You know what to do. Do one thing at a time. You know what's
important. And if something doesn't get done, to hell with it."

So that is what I would like to give readers of this book—the
voice of my Mom (without all the whuppin's and hard looks). My
Mom will tell you: If you have lived long enough to be an adult, and
loved enough to bring new life into the world, you have all the
potential you need to take care of that life. The rest may be trial and
error or getting advice or seeking counseling, but the potential is
there, and you have to be unafraid to tap the potential or to make
a mistake.

Mom's voice told me I could do it, and I am doing it—more or less well, but doing it.

NB: I had one advantage over some single fathers, in that I always believed I could do it. What I didn't know was what had to be done. And that's where the real shock came in: all the things you have to do—learning how to take care of things, take care of the day care, take care of each individual need, and still meet everybody's group needs. And how to divide yourself into more pieces than there can be, yet it has to be done.

The biggest problem I had to face was realizing this has to be done. Why me? Because there ain't nobody else. You're it.

I always think about this short segment in the movie *Zulu*. One of the young privates is faced with five thousand warriors coming at him, trying to kill this poor fellow—and he sees them all coming at him, just like any soldier would. He asks the sergeant there: "Why us? Why do we have to be here? Why do we have to fight 'em?" The old sergeant just looks at him: "There ain't anybody else, just us. Just do your job."

That was semi-inspirational. That's just the way you've gotta look at some things sometimes. There's no one else.

And if there is no one else, then it's up to the solo dad to set the priorities, isn't it? Or do the kids set them, or do they set themselves?

In one way, child-rearing priorities have a universal order: first love; then food, shelter, clothing, and safety; then everything else. Love comes first because all the things you do for your kids come out of your love for them. But even the next three, self-evident as they seem, can be in conflict—a single parent holding down a job to provide food and shelter may be compromising the children's safety. And what about all that "everything else"?

NB: As for setting priorities, some of them just plain set themselves. I had to be at work at certain times. Then the child care had to be taken care of, and that care had to focus on my unusual work times. Getting out of the house had to be there, 'cause I'd get into a world of trouble if I was late. I was usually standing a twelve-hour watch and relieving somebody who had been there for twelve hours. And they want to go home, just like you do at the end of your shift.

Sometimes the school things, events and programs, you can't do. You want to try to do everything, but you just can't do it.

RD: You do suddenly realize that in a lot of cases the priorities set themselves. You realize that it's more important to get them to bed so that you can get them up in the morning. You have to spend the time with them on homework because they need the help with the homework, but also because they need the time with you. And perhaps that means the dishes don't get washed tonight or at least not at a time that you would like.

I know that what I found, once I really understood the significance of the word *schedule*, is that you have to keep to it—at least loosely. Around 7:30 A.M. they all have to be up, moving, not sitting in the bed so that when you walk out of the door they can lie back down. Everybody has got to have teeth brushed and clothes on, and everybody is downstairs for breakfast at 8:00.

Then everybody has got to have dinner by 5:30 P.M. so that the bathing can start at 8:00, so that everybody can be in their bedrooms by 8:30 or 9:00 so they can all get up the next morning.

Once I got the concept of schedule and I got past the fear of whether I could do this or not, I realized that certain priorities showed up almost naturally—homework trumps chores; enough sleep can trump homework; food shopping gets more time than clothes shopping. And (a real surprise) sometimes your needs trump theirs. Of course, because I learned from both my father and my stepfather that men aren't supposed to know about these priorities, the fear was that I wouldn't know them.

Right along with fear comes that other prime motivator—guilt. Whether guilt is an emotion or not, it has a strength that can overpower any of us. Even fathers just filling in for the absent mom for a few hours can be left weak and confused because they feel guilty that they don't know what Mom knows and they are, therefore, inadequate. So what are the things to remember when guilt strikes?

NB: I think one of the most important things you want to remember about kids growing is that they are growing up and they don't have the experiences that we have. We want to make sure that we provide them with the experience. Sometimes you may have to be a little pushy with them: "Try this." "Try that." If they don't like it, don't force it, but they have to make a good try.

As parents we need to regulate the choices. Some parents I've run into, male and female, feel so guilty, they let the kids do whatever the kids want. "I'm guilty because I divorced their mom." Just because you divorced your wife does not mean you have to be overly indulgent with the kids. For one thing, the children are not going to respect you very much for it, and, for another, it's not going to be healthy for them. So give them the fair deal, and everything will work out better.

Trying to overcompensate by whatever means for the loss of the other parent is a very real issue. It's very hard to deal with. And sometimes you may not know that you're overcompensating.

Kids need limits, just like liquid needs a glass to be put in so that it will stay in one place. Kids need to have the same kind of limits around them so that they know where their boundaries are. And you want to let them grow up, give them choices, and let them learn responsibility in keeping with their abilities at each age.

RD: Feeling guilty seems to be a human birthright. We like to pretend that it has an ethnic or religious flavor: Catholic guilt, Jewish guilt, Black mother guilt. But as far as I can tell, it really infects us all.

If you are dealing with children, you will feel guilt—guilt because they cried, guilt because they didn't cry. Feeding, punishment, play, sleep, TV, video games, adult social life, child social life—every inter-action between you and the children holds the potential for guilt.

I think that's because you are cast as the big guy in the car-toon—everything you do with the little guy can be too strong, too mean to the little guy. It's easy to say, "Deal with it," but at least here is a clue: The only things you should really feel guilty for are hurting your child and not acting out of love. That means disappointing the kid, making a mistake, and bringing on tears or not drying them are not reasons for guilt. But if you don't love the kids or you truly injure them, it's time to seek help or other child-rearing arrangements.

NB: I think when you get into the position of being a single dad you have a lot of things to deal with, not the least of which is the guilt of being a single parent. You know that the children are suffer-ing, and you feel guilty about that and want to make it up to them.

Let's deal with a specific guilt issue. How about feeding the children?

RD: Food is a real issue for me. I guess it's the most direct con-nection to the word *nurturing*. Nurturing a child is essential, yet in our society it is not something that men do or are expected to do. And finding something for them to eat is not nearly as difficult as find-ing something they *will* eat. As you are acknowledging that every-body will eat something, you still must make sure that something touches all the various food groups sometime during the day.

Letting them eat late, even healthy, snacks though they haven't finished the dinner you made; trying to give them choices without winding up serving them cake and ice cream every night—all of those issues have come up real quick in my solo dad time, and we'll discuss them further later. But whether it's for an afternoon or the rest of their lives, you'll run into it. If it's an afternoon, I think many fathers tend to say, "Give the kid whatever she wants. Let her mother deal with the upset stomach when she gets her back." That's not fair to her mother, and, fair or not, it's not fair to the child. You are supposed to be a parent; you have to take care of her. You should be providing something that is not going to damage her health, even if it's short-term damage.

NB: But when you're looking at a four- or five-year-old, the question shouldn't be "What do you want for breakfast?" or "Are you hungry? Do you want breakfast?" but rather "Do you want the cold cereal or the frozen pancakes?" That is, if you give them any choice at all—"Here's breakfast." Or put even more simply, cook up some sausage and put it on the table, heat up some pancakes, and put a box of cereal out. You can give them a choice, but you need to limit it, or else you're going to have a meal that goes on for hours, and everybody is going to get upset.

You need to have expectations for them constantly, and when they've met them, give them a new set so they'll be challenged. If they're not challenged, they're not going to grow very much.

Setting limits also means enforcing them, and any parent who has once locked horns with a child will vouch for the validity of the question "Why is it so hard?"

NB: I read somewhere that children have one full-time job: they need to find out where the parent is weak and then exploit that weakness. The parent has several other full-time jobs, and you as a parent can devote only part of your time to each, and you need to have your jobs work the first time. But the kids will sit there all day or all week in an effort to break up what you have put together.

And that's the really tough part, because you have to hold the line. If you do this early enough and consistently enough, you build a pattern of behavior to where limits are a manageable issue. And the child is going to grow better for it in the long run, better than if he or she is given free rein.

And you can't let certain children have choices, because they're too young to have that much responsibility.

So when are they old enough to take responsibility?

RD: That's one that I feel more than a little uncomfortable with. I come from a family in which there was a divorce when I was about five. My mother had certain things that she did and certain things that she left for my stepfather to do. Most of the domestic duties were divided between her and my older sister.

When I listen to you talk about letting the older kids do chores, I realize I have this tremendous difficulty in letting my oldest (or any of my children) take care of things. Part of it is that Mike does occasionally appear to be more than a little irresponsible, though he has always been one who has looked out for and tried to help his younger siblings.

Well, I discovered this summer that he wants to wash dishes and wash clothes and mow the lawn and cook. And I'm saying, "But he's only twelve." And I talk to my sister, and she says, "But I was doing it when I was only twelve." For me, that's still a real hill to climb over.

I have been continually asking, "Am I making them do too much?" And if I look at it honestly, I'm not making them do nearly enough. None of them. Paul tells the baby-sitter, "I'm a little guy. I shouldn't have to do that." And Andrea sets up deals where she's going to "trade" her duties with her older brother and then doesn't do his and doesn't do hers either.

At least I know I'm not alone in this. A 1996 study released by Ohio State University discovered that husbands are doing more household duties, but wives aren't doing any less. How is that possible? Well, it is possible because dads are taking up the duties the children used to have. Parents these days are so pleased that their kids are going to school, that they are not on dope or in gangs or driving drunk or likely to be shot. Parents are so pleased that their kids aren't in trouble, the parents will take on any job that is outside of staying good and making grades.

Many of us have lost the point I've heard comedian Chris Rock make—that not being a criminal is not something to be proud of. You are expected to be good, and then other praiseworthy behavior is required on top of that.

But, as we said with priorities, it is often circumstance that makes us change our ways. I recently went through a period with no baby-sitter, and the kids had to watch out for themselves and do some chores to help out. It's true, things got forgotten, like our poor dog's afternoon walk. But we got things done, we got fed, we got our homework finished—Paul even got better grades.

That has made me think hard about ever getting another regu-lar sitter. I realize that I was using the sitter as a sort of crutch: If she wasn't getting the kids to do chores (And why should she? They weren't her kids), then obviously I was too busy to get them to do chores. Instead I either yelled my head off as they finally did one thing out of five, or I did the chores.

NB: I think, if I could go back, I would push a schedule and absolute duties a little bit more. Require that they be done and take the time to, if necessary, stand over them and stay up late until they finished it. That way, they would know "I can do it now when it's early and I've still got time to do other things, or I can stay up late, and Dad's gonna stand there totally POed at me 'cause I didn't get it done when I was supposed to." I slipped in a lot of those areas with the older boys as far as getting things done went.

RD: Don't we all?

Priorities, limits, responsibilities, enforcement—add them to that first list of love, food, and shelter, and you've got quite a job. To get a big job done, you have to get organized. So, are you organized? You may be more organized than you ever suspected.

RD: My form of organization is managing to remember just in time to get it done. That has always worked for me. But I'm getting older, and the internal clock is running down. Sometimes the men-tal alarm rings an hour late, and sometimes it doesn't ring at all.

One of the hardest things for me is getting organized in the traditional sense of organization. I lost an hour at home one morning, and I missed a meeting. I told myself it was because I couldn't find my wallet, but the truth is, I was late because I couldn't remember when the appointment was, despite the fact that I had written it down in my calendar software. Organization isn't always good for me.

But I have found that going to grad school has helped. I realized over the last two years that there is no way I can get all of this done without thinking out what I have to do today, when I can do it, and how I can combine trips without missing deadlines.

I always have a load of clothes in the washer or dryer and dishes in transition from sink to dishwasher to pantry. All that "woman's work" is done just like the old saying implies—around the clock and whenever I'm passing through the room with an idle second. I cook a couple of nights a week now, and I do my groceries once a week in ten minutes on the computer—except for when I have to go out for what I forgot.

I find I start thinking about what I'm going to do for the next eight to twelve hours, not at the same time every day but at a particular time in the day. I might do it while I'm getting the kids up, because that tends to be a long process in this house. While I'm getting them together, I'm getting myself together to go to work. During that time I'm thinking that I need to get my shirts together to go to the laundry. I need to stop off at the discount store because they have a sale on toilet paper or bookshelves, and I need to take my shoes in for new heels. I need to stop off at the bank. On the way home, I need to get dinner, or I can do what I did not do this morning, and I have to get these things in the mail because, once I get home, it's going to be homework time. After I've finally gotten my three to bed, and during that time before I have gotten myself to bed, I'm thinking about what I'm going to do the next morning. I'm not writing things down, but I am making mental notes and using them to help me through the rest of the day.

NB: Some people are very organized, and they extend that organization to the kids. There are some inhuman elements of not being flexible, but there is a lot to be said for having a schedule. But I am a fairly organized person.

RD: I'm a functional disorganized person. I rarely forget stuff to where I've completely blown it, but I spend an awful lot of wasted time and effort catching up and getting hold of things because I have not planned them out completely.

NB: Organization, like much of single parenting, is something that takes time to learn. I still struggle with it. I can get organized on specific tasks, such as doing grocery shopping. Planning has to be done all of the time. It takes time, and as I continue to do this, I will learn more.

What I am able to do is, at certain areas I can be a little organized on the fly, as in grocery shopping, and that's because I'm a little more in tune with cooking. I like to eat good food and have a good meal without a lot of things going on, so when I'm shopping I have in mind what I am going to do with meals for the next two weeks.

Organization is a long-term thing. Organization is not my strong point. There are a couple of people who, if anyone were to say that I'm organized, would fall on the floor laughing. You know what you are going to get, you know what you are going to cook. You are organized in the things that you like to do.

All this talk of getting ready may make you feel a little tense, a bit anxious, ready to scream. How can you do all this and remain calm and rational? Well, the truth is, sometimes you can't. This leads to something called the *bad dad*.

RD: Something that is part of my philosophy is that there's got to be room for "Bad Dad." Dad can't be good all the time. Dad can't be Ward Cleaver or Cliff Huxtable or whatever his name was on "Father Knows Best." There are times when logic is not working, when quiet conversation or a smart line or even a quiet but direct command is not working, that Dad has got to be able to say, "I said do it NOW!"

Yet I think that I have exercised my vocal cords far too much. I realize that Bad Dad's got to be there. It's just that so many times I find myself at the office or on the way home, thinking, "Why did I do that? Wasn't there some other way or some better way? Why do I seem to fall back on loud voices and 'Go to your room and stay there' so often?"

And yet I'm not sure that it's not something that everybody has to do "so often." Maybe I'm doing a lot better than I think. And I think I'm doing a lot better than what a lot of those talk-show guest experts would have us believe.

We have to deal with the challenges as they come in our own ways. Obviously, one cannot break the law. Obviously, one must love one's children. And when you do that, you don't do things to damage the child. I often wonder if I'll wind up being the subject of *Daddy Dearest*. But Daddy had to get you up and out of bed, and if that meant I had to put the toothbrush in your hand and make you stand there with tears in your eyes and brush, Daddy had to do it.

C h a p t e r   2

Care and Feeding

Buying, cooking, teaching, entertaining—these basic duties can define the job of solo dad. The problem is, though you have probably dealt with all of them as an adult, you have been handling them for yourself and not for one or two or more squirming masses preprogrammed to mumble, "Don't like it," and rush off into their own little world.

Parenting is an adventure in humility, but there are a few tricks in the dad bag that can help you reach a sort of bemused success.

So, ready or not, here they come. Time to roll up the sleeves and dig into that bouncing bundle of trouble and fun; taking care of your child.

Such as, how do you shop for children?

RD: One of my first challenges, and it's continuing, is learning how to shop for a child. I know by now that what I buy has nothing to do with what a twelve-year-old will wear or a nine-year-old will eat. And I know I must actually get the kids away from the toys, away from the videos and other stuff, so that they can say, "Yeah, I want to wear that. Cool."

But my first solo dad year, when they were five, seven, and nine, I found that I'd pick up stuff that they couldn't wear. It drives me insane that jean companies think it's so cute to provide button-fly, button-waist jeans in five-year-old sizes that five-year-olds can't get off when they have to go to the bathroom at school. The clothing companies design wonderful little one-piece outfits for girls, but they don't have a zipper, so the girl has to take the whole thing off for a potty break.

Knowing about those things didn't come naturally or easily for me. I wasted a lot of money on clothes they wore once because they had to embarrass themselves or ask the teacher to free them from the clothes. Some of these clothes should come with a chastity belt key.

NB: My experience on this kind of thing: I steered the kids, telling them, "Never mind fashion; we need function," and looked for it. I tried to keep up with the very good brand names. Health-Tex and Osh-Kosh have clothes that are designed for kids, and you need to look at that. But a lot of times you can't find these things around, or they may not be priced where you can afford them. But if you can compare what you remember was on the top-brand clothes, you can look for it in the off brands.

Or you can try the clothing resale shops; it seems like only the best clothes last long enough for resale once the kids grow out of them.

Still, it's very frustrating with some of the clothes for kids. But I think this is kind of universal—there are some adult clothes that leave you wondering how you are expected to wear that and function.

I gave the kids pretty much leeway in choosing clothes. I guided them, and there were times I flat out said no. When they were younger—four, five, and six—it was more my decision than theirs.

As they got into the preteen years and early adolescence, I would ask, "What do you want?" and unless it was something really outlandish, I'd go with it. That gives them a nice transition into making their own decisions, and it also lets you get them a wardrobe they actually will wear.

The short-term, weekends-with-kids fathers should seriously consider what clothes they buy for children, even when it's a rare or special occasion.

RD: Even short-term, weekend dads need to pay attention to this. You can, of course, go out and buy that thing that is totally impractical that the kid wants, but let me suggest that weekend dads keep it at home and let the kid wear it at your place. It gives you a little bit of peace. Otherwise you may have to deal with its going to someone else's house, and you have to hear about it, or, even worse, it disappears.

When, so often, it seems that doing it yourself will save time and frustration, do you have to shop *with* them to shop *for* them?

RD: I have finally learned to drag the kids away from the other distractions in the department store, to have them try things on and to approve the purchases. Solo dad life is too short to do time in the returns line. And not having their opinion, unless they are as consistent as taxes, will cost you dearly.

I even learned this year to wait until school starts, if I can, for the word from fashion-conscious junior high school. I sent Mike to school in his sixth-grade pants and held on to a few bucks, and within a week he was saying, "The skinny pants have to go, Dad. Everybody laughs 'cause I don't wear wide-legs." It made it much more pleasant going out for what he wanted, and I also took him by himself and went to a store that sold only clothes, to cut down on distractions.

Every experience is a lesson. Every mistake costs enough in money, time, or self-esteem—none of which you have enough of if you are raising children—that you don't ever want to make that mistake again.

Many school districts now mail out lists each summer detailing the numerous school supplies that parents are supposed to assemble before the first bell rings. It is like outfitting an army, and discount stores turn into war zones in late July and early August as families march through the aisles, seeking that illusive red, erasable pen. What are the rules for supply buying?

RD: One of the things you have to realize: You have to take them with you when you go school shopping. You can't run off like you did to the hardware store and browse the aisles and say, "Hmmm, I like this, and I'll throw in that." A lot of the school supplies—backpacks and pencil boxes and lunch boxes—you better let them pick, because they won't take it if they don't have some say in what it looks like.

NB: You know, when you're in this supposedly unusual situation of the single parent, you often have the feeling that you need to do more. You need to do the job of two; you need to fill in for that missing parent, and you wind up filling in for that child as well.

So it might be easier for me to go through that whole list of school supplies and pick up and read the packages and make sure that they are the right things, but it's not teaching the child anything.

And now, another lesson in delegating responsibility.

NB: Well, what I like to do is give the list to the kids. This actually came out of frustration, when I didn't know what to get. "You can read it; you're in charge. You're responsible for getting your supplies—get 'em."

They now have a responsibility; they have to complete that. And it's a simple one. And they know how. "All my friends are getting this, and I need this kind of paste and that kind of a marker."

Of course, you have to check, and you have a chance for a learning experience here, too. They grab some markers that aren't the right kind. "OK, your list says this kind of marker, but now you have to look on the marker and see. You see here, it says this isn't the right kind of marker." "Oh."

Now you've done something else, and this is something you are going to see, a theme throughout, is teaching the children to be good shoppers, and teaching them a little bit of economics with regard to how they're purchasing things. You can give them a budget and say, "Here's some money to get supplies, but if you get this, you're going to have some money left over, and there's candy on the way out."

And as simple as this lesson sounds, you're now teaching these kids at the six-, seven-, and eight-year-old level the value of a dollar. And this is something they're going to be able to keep with 'em. A lot of kids don't get this when Mom or Dad goes out and then says, "Here's your stuff" (poof!).

RD: Six, seven, or eight? I'm still trying to get started at ten, eleven, and thirteen. As the new guy on the block in this, I can listen to it and say, "Why didn't I do that?" It's important.

But, just at the end of the '97 school year, I took the kids toy shopping. I said, "You have a certain dollar limit, and just like 'The Price Is Right,' you can hit it, but you can't go over. If you go over, I take two of the things you wanted and I take them back. And if you go under, you don't get the money that you go under." And Andi sat there, hands on her knees and a sad look on her face, trying to add when it was $7.99 and 2 bucks. But she worked through all of the things she needed to do to finally come out close to what she had to spend.

A little side clue: Looking for an inexpensive reward for your child? Try a pencil.

RD: This my ex taught me, that little things like decorated pencils can be useful, especially as rewards. Pencils with unusual designs or sports teams' colors printed on the wood give kids real pleasure—

as opposed to adults, who have to see that Mont Blanc star on the tip. This lesson has expanded so that I now know I can give my daughter a card for Easter or Halloween, and she'll love it as much as a toy. Well, almost as much.

Feeding the beast (or beasts) is a subject that could devour this book and several others. But its importance is underlined by the many issues springing from it, such as the guilt factor, how to shop, health, and safety, and how (or even whether) to cook.

RD: As I said earlier in this book, my most guilt-ridden issue is feeding the kids. And what I've found after five years of this is that I let their taste dictate to me, up to a point.

Now, part of that is because when I was a kid, not too long after I got out of junior high school, my mother didn't seem to care whether we ate what she cooked. In fact, she didn't really want to cook. We would take our allowance and go out and buy dinner. There were a number of fast-food places within walking distance, so we would go out and buy fast food and live off that for the evening, and our mother said, "I don't care."

How our author survived is another question, but there are health issues to be considered, aren't there?

RD: What I learned, at a real cost, when I first began feeding my kids on my own is that this process is not like that experiment I was once told of, where they put all different kinds of foods on the table and let the kids roam free through the room. Supposedly, after a period of time, all the children will have eaten a balanced diet because they will get tired of all of that chocolate and want a Brussels sprout now and then.

No way, not true.

I wound up in the hospital with Andrea, and with Paul moaning and groaning on the bathroom floor in my house, before I realized they were taking in no fiber, and when they take in no fiber, their bodies don't get anything out. They got very constipated. They were eating oatmeal in the morning, but cereal just wasn't enough. I had to find ways of getting them to eat vegetables. So I don't agree with the suggestions that if you let the kids go on their own, they will eventually eat a balanced meal.

NB: I would disagree with any study like that, and I'd bet it was done before junk food. That means you are stuck with a study that's based on putting a whole lot of good food out there, and the kids eventually will go out and eat a balanced diet. Well, yeah, if there is nothing else to eat. But if you put out junk food, they will gorge themselves on that.

But what's the trick to getting green things down young throats?

RD: What I wind up doing is making two or three vegetables almost every meal. With three kids, there is always one who doesn't like what the other two are having. So it may be peas and green beans or green beans and broccoli or broccoli and corn. And I do season them, because they still don't believe they can season food themselves so that it is edible.

Kids' tastes change with the wind, and most of the time you can't figure out why. It is like some random particle beam zaps them in the back of the head—"You will no longer eat chicken." But you sometimes can affect it. It used to be Michael and now it's Andrea who will try something new, especially if Dad is eating it. "Oh, what are you eating? Can I try some?" Paul will put his tongue on it. I don't know that he can feel it, much less taste it, but he will just touch it with his tongue. Then again, Paul, forever known as Dr. No, likes nothing except a plain hot dog.

I do a lot of fast-food buying, I must confess, and I try to supplement it with some fiber, fruit, or vegetables.

NB: Feeding kids is a very interesting challenge, especially if you don't like to cook. The first thing I would have to say for any single dad is to decide at some point you are going to have to cook, and you might as well learn how to do it right. And there are a lot of very simple things you can do.

The authors have their own ideas on learning culinary skills.

NB: It's not going to happen overnight, especially if you haven't cooked before. But if you can get a good basic cookbook and just start reading it, most people who can read can learn to cook. Just do a little bit at a time. My favorite is a Betty Crocker cookbook.

RD: I get my Fannie in the kitchen—*The Fannie Farmer Cookbook*, that's my favorite. But you may still have to talk me down from the ledge if my egg whites won't whip or my cheese sauce clots.

NB: I like to cook. I cooked an entire Irish Christmas dinner, right from the appetizers to dessert, for a party last December. I taught myself to cook a long time ago, when I was still in high school. I've been trying to teach my kids how to cook, teach them some of the things I've learned and let them cook, and we can each take turns. At eleven years old, Karl was able to cook an entire meal if I wrote the recipes down and told him what to do by himself. Now that he's on his own, he can cook a lot better and feeds himself well instead of going out a lot.

RD: Mike likes to cook. There is nothing wrong with men cooking. We get caught up in these silly ideas of what men do and what men don't do. Obviously, the best-known chefs in the world are men. I've discovered a lot of men that I meet like to cook, though few of them cook for a big family. Probably there are others who would enjoy it if they took the time.

Choosing what to cook, beyond your own tastes or your child's interests, takes some learning, too.

NB: I look at labels because I found that there are some surprises out there. Stuff that is supposed to be good, you find out, isn't quite as good as you thought it was.

RD: My question for you then is: Where do you find the time? Everything of course for us boils down to time.

NB: Start in the produce section. Introduce the kids to fresh cooked vegetables here and there. You can do that, and sometimes they just like raw stuff. How do you keep it from going bad? You don't buy very much, so you go to the store a little more often. Or you can find out what kind of fruits they like.

RD: Fruit was the easiest thing. They eat a lot of fruit, I guess because of the sugar in it, but at least I know that it's healthier than processed foods.

NB: Well, it tastes good and it does have that sugar in it. But you're starting out with a good basic allowance there. As for reading the labels, once you get into your boxes and your prepared sauces and everything else, I just did that a little bit at a time. Sometimes I spend more time at it than others, and sometimes I don't have time.

The trick is to learn how to read labels quickly. There is a knack to knowing how to read labels, knowing that the ingredients are listed in order of quantity. The first ingredient is what there's the most of, and so on.

The nutrition labeling has gotten a little bit better. I look to try to keep the fat down, and if it's going to have fat in it, keep that fat down to the unsaturated fat. Then look at sugars and sodium.

You learn to do a little bit at a time. You can't do it all at once. Just start looking at some labels here and there, and there are some very simple comments and guidelines that you look for. I've been looking at labels for years.

Now that we are back in the store aisles, any other tips about shopping? How about coupons? Aren't they a good idea?

NB: I avoid coupons for the most part. Most of the time, when I used to do coupons, I'd go through them saying, "I'm going to save some money here. I will save thirty cents here, fifty cents there." And what I found was happening was the coupons were deciding what I was going to buy. I don't like to do that because you wind up spending more money and you don't always get the quality of food that you want.

I know some people who are religious about coupons. This is a ritual with them and part of their lives. I don't want to spend my time looking at the food store coupons.

I also try to limit myself to stuff that I would normally buy when I was buying groceries and there was a mom in the house. I didn't worry about prices; I didn't think about them.

So how about generic foods?

NB: I used to try to look for generic this and generic that and get the lower price, but I also noticed that you do get lower quality. Now, in some cases it's negligible, so it's not a big problem, but sometimes you get stuff that really isn't that good, and I don't think it's a good food value.

Is there anything you can do to save some pennies?

NB: You look at the unit price. I drive my daughter crazy with this—compare this one or that one. This is a different size, and it looks like it's a better price, but if you compare the unit price, this one is the better deal.

And Nick has a recipe for combining food value with financial value.

NB: Take spaghetti sauce. I don't like to get a lot of sugar in it, and if you look at most of your prepared spaghetti sauces, there is a lot of sugar of one type or another. It may just say *sugar* or it may just say *corn syrup* (which is sugar) or *dextrose* (which is sugar). There sure are a lot of different ways to say *sugar* without saying *sugar*. Avoid sugar in a lot of your prepared foods if at all possible because sugar is used primarily as a filler, and it gets you craving it.

But, getting back to the spaghetti sauce, a sixteen-ounce bottle of a name-brand sauce might cost you $2 to $4. But you can buy a sixteen-ounce can of Hunt's spaghetti sauce—traditional, no sugar added, no salt added, just a simple basic sauce—and it's under $1. And I can take that—it's ready to go—and dump it in a pot. I'll add my own seasonings, so I'm adding a few extra cents to it, to give it the flavor I want. I may chop up some onions or green peppers or maybe even chop up a tomato. For about $1, I've got a sauce that I think is far better in quality and nutrient value than the higher-priced brand.

And there are a lot of things out there like that. You have to begin to look at the food and not pay attention to the hype. You have to become a label reader. All the information is there, but you don't want to try to learn it all at one time, because you'll never do it that way.

There is that subject of time again. Any clues to how to reduce grocery shopping time?

NB: I had the advantage of being a military reservist, so I was able to go to the commissary, and I would plan to go once a month, and I'd spend $300 or more, so we'd be in the commissary or supermarket shopping for at least two hours. When the kids got a little bit older and I found I had too many other things and we lived too far from the commissary, I still wouldn't do a major shopping trip more often than every two weeks, and I would spend an hour or so doing the shopping.

RD: I have to say I marvel at your memory. I could not possibly go to the grocery store once or twice a month, because, as soon as I go home, I'd discover, "Oh, I forgot the cookies, the eggs, the soap."

One thing that I have come to use is a computer-based grocery-ordering service. It is something that is offered on the Internet, though there are still grocery stores that will take your orders over the phone and fill them. But these Internet services are spreading across the country.

Before I shop, I will go through my list—on the service I use, shopping lists for past weeks can be called up easily—and that gives me ideas of what I need for this week. I also wander through the house and say, "Yeah, I need this and I need the other." And I can bring the kids over to the computer, and they will tell me what they want. It's really great. I could not have lived without it when I was in grad school, and I don't want to live without it now.

NB: Well, I make a general list so I don't have to go shopping so often. Walk into your kitchen and think about what you eat, what you are going to eat, what is not in the refrigerator or on the shelves. Once the kids are about ten years old, you start asking them to check the kitchen for items. That gets the kids involved, and they will help to remind you.

Another thing to do when trying to make out a list: Remember how the store is set up and make your shopping list like that. It makes it easier for you to do your shopping because you are not looking all over your list and running back and forth across the store.

Now, while looking at the cupboards, you can do something backward here, too. When you look at your cupboards, see what you are out of and what you are not out of. Once something has been sitting there, waiting for someone to eat it for the last six months, strike it off your list permanently.

RD: I remember once my stepfather gave me some smelt that a friend of his had caught. That smelt went through three moves, three different refrigerators and apartments, and finally we just looked at each other and said, "Why are we carrying this around? We are never going to eat it." So, after years in frost-free limbo, we finally threw it out.

Oh, while you were in the store, you picked up cleaning supplies, didn't you? Of course you did. So what are you going to do with them, and when?

RD: As I implied before, work in the house is never really done. You can't look at it as a task that must be finished, and then you move on to the next one. Once you've cleaned the bathroom, you still have to go back and clean it again.

Since most of us guys are blissfully unaware of what house-keeping is about, here's one tip: it's about having a place your kids' friends don't mind visiting, a place you don't have to kick your way into, a place that is comfortable and not condemned by the board of health.

A second tip: Housework, like the house itself, is a family thing. Since many of us figured that not dumping the Sunday paper on the floor was our contribution to a sparkling home, we may not readily know that keeping house has enough jobs to go around. And it is good to have those jobs go around to everyone in the household. Doing chores is a child's introduction to the working world, but, even more, it's a child's physical contribution to the family.

Chores can start at just about any age. If they are old enough to mess a room up, they are old enough to clean up after themselves. Just remember two things that I tend to forget: the kids respond best when you clean up along with them, and they need a place to put the toys, drawings, toy parts, torn drawings, and other assorted detritus of play. Discount stores are continually having sales on plastic boxes big enough to store the *Titanic*'s iceberg enemy. Buy some and place them strategically around your home, or else keep the kids playing near the boxes. Of course, you must remember that the kids will probably prefer to pour out the toys onto the floor and play in the boxes.

As they get older and in school, they can take on family-wide chores: collecting trash from the wastebaskets, piling newspaper into the recycling bin, sweeping, putting dishes into or pulling them out of the dishwasher, taking out the trash, walking the dog. As they grow even older, they can wash dishes or clothes, mop, vacuum, and cook. And when they get as old as you, they can do what you should be doing—a little bit of all of this.

You can schedule the kids' duties—I like to have them start just before homework time, after they've had a snack and cooled out from school.

However, you can't truly schedule your own duties. There are going to be spills the children can't clean up, times when you would rather have them study and you rinse the dishes, and far too many duties for all of them to handle, especially if you are solo dadding over an extended period.

From my vast experience, I have noted two main styles of house-cleaning: those who stay in one room until it is finished and those who wander from room to room, changing jobs as they change location. I am in transition—I used to be a dedicated wanderer, letting the book I found in the kitchen carry me to the living room, where I found the bills, which I carried to my desk, where I found trash that took me to the kitchen, and. . . . But now I try to stay in one room so that I can say that I finished at least one spot before I collapsed.

I still let my travels carry me into jobs, so that I always have a load of clothes in the washer or dryer, a load of dishes soon to be washed or ready to be shelved, and I do those things in the off moments I have.

And, though I have no schedule, I try to make sure that the kitchen floor gets mopped at least once a week, the beds and tow-els are changed on that schedule, the rugs are vacuumed at least every other week, the table and counter tops are washed off after the evening meal. There will be Days of Major Effort when I tackle clean-ing under the boy's bunk beds or my desk, but that tends to be sea-sonal, if not timed to the leap year.

Housework yields to homework, which we discovered was a truly touchy subject. In fact, we are so heated over it, we'd rather save it for a separate book. Look for *How to Fight Your Kids' School* if our publishers are willing to take another chance on this. But here are a few brief ideas on perpetuating educational efforts at home.

NB: I'll look at the kids' homework, but I expect them to get it done. I know some parents who check the homework every night. I don't. Parents can't have a life and do that.

RD: I may spend too much time with the kids' homework. When I was in grad school, I found we couldn't all sit down and do our work together. Dad had to first separate the three of them so that each one wouldn't keep another one screaming with laughter, in tears, or otherwise distracted. Then I spent the next two hours circling through the house, checking to see who had problems and who was still distracting himself. (Not herself; only the hims distracted themselves in my house.) To get my work done, I had to go to bed at the same time the kids did, then wake up at 4:00 or 5:00 A.M. to get my studying in.

But if you believe in education, you have to believe homework time is a priority. And remember that it is also one of those rare times when you can interact directly with each of your children.

Housekeeper, homework expert, chief cook, and body washer—their hygiene is also one of your jobs. Proper instruction can go a long way to taking this dirty job out of your hands, but early on you still need to supervise everything from baths to hair brushing to make sure they are getting it right.

When they take responsibility for their own upkeep depends on their own maturity, but also what physical attributes they have to deal with. For example, Nick's daughter was brushing her hair herself in early elementary school, while Reg still does the occasional coif for his darlin' with the very curly locks. And even into junior high school, a brief word is needed to remind a child to brush the teeth before bed or wash that hair tonight.

NB: Actually, once my kids were getting around thirteen or four-teen, it was automatic. You know when you smell. Clean yourself.

I know that around five or six, a child figures, "Who cares how dirty I am? I certainly don't. I don't care whether I stink. My friends don't care whether I stink. We are all digging in the mud, pulling friends through the trash. We don't care what we look like. What do you mean, brush my hair? I don't find any value in that." Then they get older, and friends' opinions matter a lot more.

RD: But there are, on occasion, other issues: Because hygiene is important, we all agree that it's important. But because it's important to Dad, I can use it to leverage him when I want some other kind of attention. I don't always realize when the routine is going on. Even-tually I begin to realize that it's not that they don't want to take a bath or brush their teeth, but that there is something else that needs attention.

Just recently, Mike tried to convince me that he had already had his shower. "I got up when no one else was up, and I took my shower," he mumbled into the far side of the bed. This from the resident log who won't roll over for the first two wake-up calls. But it was hours later when I realized that he didn't want to smell good since he was under orders to talk to teachers about work he had not done. The shower story was his way of saying he didn't want to face the music.

Hopefully, other dads can be quicker on the pickup when this is happening.

You are also responsible for meeting medical needs when kids are in your care. But how can you tell when it is time to call the doctor, call off work, or just call off school?

RD: My kids never seem to have a fever above ninety-nine. I have had times, when they were really sick, when I sent them to school and discovered later they were really sick. There are times when I've kept them home and about an hour later realized they weren't sick at all. Though it may seem really simple and that anybody should know this, men are not thought of as nurturers, and they are not encouraged to be. So they have less practice with sick kids and may not know what the signs are.

NB: One thing I can recommend—go down, check with the American Red Cross, and find out when they have CPR classes and basic first aid classes. Among the best lessons you will learn is what questions to ask, how to ask them, and how to determine if an answer is real or if it's made up.

Also, you can get a good medical reference book.

RD: Actually, here is something that a lot of men don't know—they may have Dr. Spock around, and there are chapters in *Dr. Spock's Baby and Child Care Book* on identifying childhood diseases: Is this chicken pox, or is it rash?

NB: A good medical reference is a good thing to have around the house. And, once you find one, don't be afraid to use the darn thing. You may not be a doctor, but you are not as dumb as you might think you are. Don't be afraid to pick the thing up and look through and make some kind of decision. Also, if you've got a computer, you can get some good medical reference programs with all sorts of information and color graphics, which give even better depictions than the pictures in books.

But what are some signs of child illness?

NB: There are signs: complaining of pain when they are not feeling well. When they are babies, it's really hard to tell. If you have a child who doesn't really want to go to school, knowing that is also very important.

RD: Knowledge of your child is crucial. Andrea wants to go to school, so when she's complaining that she's sick, there is a pretty good chance that she is sick. She also gets inconsolable and cries. Paul would rather do just about anything than go to school, so occasions come up when he thinks he's going to pull one over on Dad, and he will whine about a pain in his shoulder or a sick stomach.

NB: I like to feel the head and, if it feels hot, I have to take it into consideration that they have just gotten out of bed and it's going to feel warm, or they have been up and out a little while and they are still hot. How they look, how the eyes focus, whether they are lethargic or not; it seems simple, but I know a lot of dads who don't know for sure. The truth is that you don't always know the truth about whether a kid is sick.

RD: One of the things I do to help me determine whether they are sick or not is to say, "I understand you're not feeling well right now, but I need you to get up and put your clothes on, brush your teeth, and try to eat some breakfast." If they can do that, they are not sick enough to stay at home. But they may get up and get their clothes on and not be able to go down for breakfast. Or they may not be able to get their clothes on. That way you can tell if they really are sick and not just too sleepy because they stayed up late watching "The Simpsons." Trying to get started is a good way of finding out whether they can keep going.

NB: You can look at the throat. Aren't throats lovely to look at? There is a way to look at throats. Get a flashlight and look down there and try to avoid using a tongue depressor. You look at the back of the throat. (Actually, it's a good idea to look when the kid is healthy, so you have a reference point.) Do you see a lot of red darkness in the back? That is usually a sign of an infection. You are getting a lot of blood pulsing up there trying to deal with that infection, and the skin is tender, and the nerve endings are more sensitive. It probably is an infection; you probably need to go see the doctor.

Or see if there is a lot of mucus coming down, a lot of drainage. Have the child take a deep breath through his or her nose. Is it stuffy?

You can try some over-the-counter medication and give it a few hours to work. If that doesn't work, you may need to call the doctor.

With all the vagueness, should you send a sick child to school, or occasionally keep a well child at home?

RD: I have been told of a doctor whose medical procedure was to send his kids to school anyway. "You are going to have to go through that cold anyway. No medicine is going to cure it; the disease has to run its course."

I'm not one who believes that if you're ill you should still go on to school. Michael, until this year, missed a week of school every year, a full week plus whatever other days, from catching a cold. With his asthma, I wasn't willing to risk more serious illness. You give that cold to everyone else, and it may come back to you a few months later. I don't think that you learn much by going to school sick. There is no learning going on.

If you have the children for an extended period, more serious ailments are likely to arise. When should you call for expert advice?

RD: I am one who thinks you should call the doctor at the beginning and ask questions if you feel uncomfortable about something with your child's health. You will learn soon enough that there are things you don't need to call the doctor about. And in all cases, if a child has been ill five days, I call in the troops.

NB: I've had occasions where I haven't had much faith in what the doctors were saying, or they just didn't leave me with the feeling that they had given my kid good treatment. I am all for learning about these things yourself. And a lot of the stuff you've learned, you had to learn, like how to tell a genuine complaint from a phony complaint. Kids are good actors, but there is usually a flaw. In fact, sometimes you can tell when a kid is trying to fake it because the kid will keep saying, "It's really bad! I'm gonna die!" That's a contraindicator: they are not really sick; they just don't want to get up and go to school. And when you do take them to the doctor, grill the doctor. Find out what the doctor looked for. You are training yourself. Don't be afraid to handle it. Men are competent, too.

But dealing with an ill child may be nothing in comparison to the logistical problems when your child is ill and no child care is available. Perhaps the most useful tactic in this case is summed up in one word: *honesty.*

RD: When children are ill when you are at work, it's a big problem. I have tried to keep it known at the school that they should call me at work, and I always let the boss know if I have to leave because one of my children is sick. I let a number of people know that I am leaving because someone is sick. Luckily, I haven't had any situation where it's so serious that someone needed me to be there immediately or someone had to be taken to the hospital.

I have on occasion had a sitter stay with sick kids. I have on other occasions stayed home myself. And there is nothing like catching kids' colds.

NB: Well, dealing with the illness can vary depending on the age group, too. When they are younger, somebody has to stay with them. I have had to take a sick child to work with me.

RD: I did that once. He threw up in my office.

NB: Well, I had to do it several times. I didn't have the leave time available to take off, and they were too young to leave home all by themselves. I would pack a sleeping bag and something for them to do and take them along, and I'd find a place in the office, back by the files or something, where they were out of the way. I'd roll out the sleeping bag and say, "Here, go to sleep."

Dealing with sick kids has been tough. Christina has been sick, and a couple of years ago when she was sick I would have to stay home. I had a woman friend who was a teacher, and if it was during summer vacation I could call and tell her that Christina was sick. "Could you come over and stay with her or take her over to your house where she can stay with you and get you and your kids sick?"

RD: A hard but necessary thing for a single dad is to get to know other parents to see what kind of network you can set up. Perhaps if one of the kids is sick, he can stay with a friend or with relatives. But I have rarely had to worry about that because I have never lived close enough to any family member who could do anything about that. It also takes a while to have some friends who are willing and able to take care of the sick child.

Just remember, not only is it OK to ask for help in this situation; sometimes it's essential. (We'll come back to this in the next chapter.)

We wanted to end this chapter on a healthier, happier note, so we chose as our last subject entertaining the children. It's a fun issue, but an issue just the same, and if you are stuck with limited finances, which children can do for you no matter what stock options you get, it can require some imagination.

RD: Folks with a lot of money may think it's easy to fly down to spend a week in Disney World, or spend $30 or $40 for the local amusement park, or go to children's plays, and on and on and on. Weekend dads and especially those who see the kids much less often than weekly will lean toward the expensive and special event. But, beyond the fact that very few parents have the kind of money to make every minute special, all those costly tickets are unnecessary. There are lots of things that can be done when you don't have the money.

Think about your own life. You may recall that week-long trip to the Grand Canyon, but when you think of your childhood, it's the several times you went fishing or the monthly excursions to the big city for movies that you recall.

A lot of what kids say they want requires some money. But you can find things that don't cost anything or are inexpensive and at the same time teach the kids valuable lessons. You are teaching them that it's not the money they like; it's what they can do with you, with or without money.

One thing to consider is public transportation. Here in Chicago, we have elevated trains that take you to the airport or to the Sears Tower or out to the suburbs. Several times I have taken the kids on the el to the airport. We wandered through the terminals. We got on the shuttle that takes you out to the long-term parking area, then rode back.

We also took the train to places that are free to the public. We went to plant conservatories. Sometimes we read at home or watched TV and discussed it.

Check for matinees. Check for free days at the museum. Check where you work or where friends work for discounts on ticket prices or admissions.

I don't know that my kids will remember my taking them to the *Star Wars* movies. But I do think they will remember going to the Garfield Park Conservatory and running through the rubber trees. Or catching the el all the way out to O'Hare. Hiking over the dunes and out to the beach at Indiana Dunes State Park. Even stopping to play at the various playgrounds in our little suburb.

NB: I used to take the kids to this amusement park in Norfolk. Their mother was in the hospital there. You could buy season tickets early in the spring when they were deeply discounted.

After that, I discovered Yorktown and Jamestown, where the first settlers landed and where Revolutionary battles were fought. Public parks and monuments. I was kind of surprised at how much the kids enjoyed these places. We also like to go camping—in state parks or even in the backyard.

RD: Also take advantage of year-round passes or memberships to various institutions in your area. Don't let childhood memories of dull Sundays in these places hold you back—most museums have learned that they must entertain if they are going to survive. They provide entertainment and are educational, all for a very low price when you stretch the membership fee out over a year.

NB: But if you get to see the kid only once a week, be careful. If you're constantly going to one museum or to the zoo, the child will begin to think Dad is very boring and has no imagination.

Sometimes a simple deck of cards can be a fun night's entertainment. You just stay home and play cards or board games, make a pizza. We used to make bread pizza. Take a piece of bread and put cheese, vegetables, meat, and tomato sauce on it. It's great and costs nothing compared to a night out.

Help!

SEEMS LIKE EVER since Cain first lifted a club to settle that fil-
ial dispute, men have been trying to go it alone in their lives.
We all want to believe we can be that sheriff, walking up that
dusty street to face our solitary fates.

But just because you are a solo dad doesn't mean you have
to do it solo.

Seeking help is never easy for us men—a sign of weakness,
even in a civilized world. But some challenges are faced better
with collaboration, and there are situations that cannot be survived without some assistance. There are plenty of times when
a law of physics—the one about being in two places at the same
time—makes it impossible to do alone all that a single parent
has to do.

This chapter deals with that assistance, especially for the physical impossibilities. (We will deal with the personal, social, and psychological needs in the last section of the book.) We know from our own lives, and feel from observing others, that this solitary road for solo dads is one chosen from fear, especially fear of showing that you are vulnerable. Well, face it, Father; you are vulnerable, and trying to grow your kids in this rocky soil will keep you vulnerable. You have the right to seek help.

So our message is simple here: Don't try to be John Wayne (especially if you don't remember him). Call for backup!

For many full-time solo dads, the first time they discover they are in deep water is when they've fallen into the straits of divorce. Custody, visitation, alimony (now called *maintenance* in some states), responsibilities for school and health, and myriad other matters tie up courts and cost small fortunes to resolve. Neither of the authors is a lawyer or a legal expert, but we have each had our own encounters with courts and other legal entities, and the one true thing we can say is that the result is never happy. The intersection of law and family is a site of damage and heartbreak. There are books that specialize in family legal matters, and there is a whole field of law for it, and we don't feel knowledgeable enough to give much advice here. But we do have testimony, here and in Chapters 4 and 6.

Here's another truth we can impart: despite all the talk and the changes in male-female relations, despite feminism and Iron John, despite *Kramer vs. Kramer* and the books, movies, and TV shows, men are not on equal footing with women in child custody deliberations.

RD: It is still very hard in divorce for the father to get custody of the children, especially if they are under twelve. So I would suspect that in most cases where the father has full custody, the wife either left, surrendered custody, or was judged to be unfit, which is exceptionally hard to prove in court. Since justice is blind, I'm sure there are cases in which a wealthy or crafty father might hoodwink a mother out of her children, but that is not the rule.

However, more judges are awarding joint custody, and here men get more equal treatment. By my divorce decree, the kids reside with me and their mother has visitation, but the declaration is one of joint parenting. My lawyer said it was the most satisfactory solution, and I am pleased with it. Still, it's not full custody.

NB: An interesting statistic, if you've got some way to research it, would be how many kids, at age thirteen, choose to live with Dad. My kids chose to live with me. My brother was divorced as soon as he got out of the navy, and his wife took their daughter. As soon as she turned thirteen, she wanted to live with her dad.

RD: I found it difficult to find hard facts on these matters. It's as if no one wants to know. But that sort of custody switch happens, for many different reasons, and especially at that adolescent age.

The legal history that came to justify maternal custody decisions is called the "tender years" philosophy. Before the turn of the century, in the old *Life with Father* days, the idea was that if there was a divorce the children stayed with the father. Of course, the divorced mom was considered a "fallen woman" anyway in those cruel times. Dad, who was often the only partner that society allowed to work for enough salary to support children, always kept the kids, until the courts came up with the "tender years" philosophy.

Starting in the 1900s, judges ruled that children younger than adolescence should stay with their mothers. This was justified by the belief that mothers were biologically and psychologically better at nurturing children. They have an innate gift, courts ruled. And until the last three decades that's the way it stayed.

It may seem that the legal system has gotten much more confusing on these issues than it was in the past, but that is mainly because the courts are getting better at dealing with individual cases and not forcing all rulings into one box. People, and especially bureaucracies, like to force you into line. The court-appointed counselor in our divorce was determined to push me into a joint custody arrangement, and she came up with a kind of two-day-switch system that would have left the kids' clothes, schoolwork, and peace of mind scattered across the Illinois landscape until all of us shouted, "I quit!" But when I got back into court, I couldn't allow myself to let the children be subjected to this. I said no to it, and it halted the proceedings in their tracks. But it also broke the ice, and we found a situation that is much more workable for all of us.

My advice for those who find themselves in this boat is to find a good lawyer. You can check the local bar association for lawyers specializing in fathers' rights. Don't let pain from a broken relationship stand in the way of your children's need to have a life with both parents, but don't let divorce deny you the right to raise your kids.

Remember that law of physics we mentioned? When you need to get to work and your kids need someone to watch them, you need that second self, someone we've now come to call a *child-care provider*.

When you are a single parent, there is no such thing as too much time. There is no such thing as enough time. And there are bound to be times when you have to be gone. Finding the right help is probably the most difficult issue all parents, single or married, face. How do you find someone who isn't banging the kids off the wall or locking them in a room when you're gone?

RD: As my marriage was breaking up, a woman who had done a lot of work in other households happened to be between jobs. She came in and provided me with the help I needed on the occasions that I needed it. Because I knew of her through acquaintances she had worked for, I had no fear of the way she operated and the kind of things she did.

I was extremely lucky. Searching for child care is very frustrating and frightening. There are a lot of avenues, but a lot of them lead to dead ends, and lots of parents have nightmare stories about what happens in those dead ends.

One set of places to look for child care is at seniors' clubs or county, township, or city organizations that assist senior citizens. There are a lot of grandmas and grandpas who would like to have something to do. There used to be a group called Operation Able in my suburb, where senior citizens signed up to get job interviews, but it disappeared recently.

You can use the Yellow Pages for child-care agencies and businesses, some where you leave the children at a center and some that will send out au pairs, nannies, or baby-sitters. Obviously, costs will range widely, as does quality of work. You could even drive around various neighborhoods—often you will see a home or business advertising child care. Or you can advertise for child care in the local paper. I was surprised that, even in good economic times, an ad brought a huge number of responses.

But the way I've found out the most about sitters and child-care givers is to talk to other people working in the business. People are not eager to turn in friends, but they are also prone to gossip and to compare their style of child care to others. They can recommend friends who might work for you.

NB: I think the first sitter I used was a thirteen-year-old girl who lived across the street, and she would come and stay overnight while I was gone. I was in the navy at the time, and her dad also was in the navy, and he understood. If she needed help, she could shout out the back door, and Mom would come over. She was pretty good at most things. It was fine, except her dad had some rules: she got a B once, and she couldn't baby-sit until she got that B up to an A. So I instantaneously lost a baby-sitter and, on very short notice, had to find someone else. So I would pack the kids up, and we'd drive to another sitter's house.

What kind of questions should you ask of potential child-care workers?

RD: The most important item you need is references. Ask for several, whether the potential sitter is from an agency or is a private care person. Ask about past experience, with names and phone numbers and the ages of the children sat for. Find out if the sitter can drive and if she has a car or needs transportation to get to work or to home. Ask about sitters' educational backgrounds, because if you use them often, they are going to have to supervise homework. Ask about styles of discipline and if they will do some housekeeping or cooking. Ask agencies and home services if they are licensed and then check the licensing agency for any complaints. You can ask about criminal records, but if that question is put to anybody but a licensing agency, there is nothing to keep them from lying. Leave money for last, as you would do at any job interview.

Another test is to pay a potential child-care worker to come while you are at home so you can see how she operates with the kids. Of course, there is the possibility the worker is going to be sweetness and light when you are there and turn into a mean old witch when you're gone. But have the sitter there for a few hours, and you should go out and come back without telling the caregiver when you will return.

What are the deciding factors over in-home or at-a-center child care?

RD: There is age of the children, trust of the child-care provider, cost, and preference. Cost is self-explanatory; trust comes from how well you know the potential child-care provider and whether you have neighbors who can help out and keep an eye on your house. Age can be contradictory—the youngest may draw out your protective instincts, yet babies and toddlers might have the easiest time in centers, where kids can make their first friends. Older kids would prefer to be where they can play with their own toys and their own friends.

NB: Early on I was faced with kids ranging from newborn baby to ten years old, and having to get day care for that and having to deal with odd hours, too. Most of your commercial day care deals with your nine-to-five job environment. And it's rare having any of them deal with infants—gotta change those diapers. They need the most care. Those are the hardest ones to find day care for.

RD: I much prefer having the care given in my house. When I was growing up, there was a time when my single mother had to have someone take care of us, and we did stop off at a woman's house right after school. But most of the time, if someone was going to sit for us, they sat in our house. I think that a child is more comfortable in his or her own home, but also I feel that if there is trouble with the sitter, the child will be more forthcoming about talking about it. Children are taught to assume that the rules are different in someone else's house.

If I couldn't keep them at home, I would go with a day-care center. It would have to be licensed, and many states set limits on the number of children that can be in a center and the number of adult workers who must be there. But state licensing, a high tuition, or a clean, well-lighted place are still no guarantees that child care will be proper and acceptable. Make surprise visits to the center and insist on touring the facilities.

We've all seen the daytime talk shows where somebody sets up a video camera and somebody is smacking somebody's kid around. You may also have witnessed, in a public place, cruel treatment of a child. But how do you really know if your child is being abused by a caregiver?

RD: One big way is just to look at your own child. Make sure that the scraped knee isn't joined by a bruise or a bump on the head when you pick up the child from day care or when you relieve the day-care worker in your home. Be careful about complaints of headaches or stomachaches when you first see your child. And, if the caregiver is working for several families, compare notes.

Another is to look at the child's behavior and listen to how the child speaks and acts, the personality that comes out. There are times, as there were times with my regular sitter, that the kids say they don't like her. So I ask further: "Why don't you like her?" You find out some-times that they don't like her enforcing the discipline that you hired her to enforce. But you have to listen and to watch.

I have a young relative whose mother realized that, when she'd pick him up after work, he would be nearly silent and morose. Once she got him home and settled, he was suddenly active, lively and talk-ative again. She realized that something happening during the day was making him withdraw and the only time he felt comfortable was at home. She had to change that situation.

However, though your most pressing question is probably "How can I be sure?" the answer is "You can't." You have to keep in the front of your mind that good child care is not a crime. Sometimes it is a necessity.

NB: If things didn't go quite right, there were some extra pressures that could be brought to bear very quickly in the military. It wouldn't be like civilian law. The military members could find themselves in the captain's office having to explain why they were hurting other peo-ple's kids. A lot of damage could be done to them real quick.

So, on that, you could go into a total stranger's house, some-body you'd never seen before, and know that your kid was going to be OK.

Even when you set up your "perfect" child-care situation—you set your rules (Reg has his posted on the living room wall) and times and salary—sometimes the best-laid schemes fit Robert Burns's poetic description. Where do you go for last-minute, emergency help when things have gone "aft agley"?

NB: What friends you do have, they may not be readily available. They may not want to. They'll help you out as long as it doesn't involve much, I found out. But when it comes down to "I need some-one to watch the kids during the midwatches next week," the response can be "Oh, well I would, but my wife's gonna wash her hair, so we can't do this." That sounds like an outlandish reason, but a lot of those reasons are along those lines. And you find out real quick that you're kind of isolated.

RD: At those times there is a need for understanding of how much friends will do. Just in January I was going to be gone for a week while getting my master's degree. I knew I was going to be gone for a week, my ex knew I was going to be gone, my regular baby-sitter knew I was going to be gone. But all of them had things to do so that they couldn't help. And I decided to give a try to all of those people who said, "Oh, if there's anything I can do. . . ." One must remember that there's a portion on the end of that sentence that you don't hear, which is "Oh, if there's anything I can do, as long as it doesn't cause too much trouble." And one shouldn't necessarily assume that people who are friends are going to go to too much trouble for you.

So at one point it looked like I was going to have my kids in three different houses for three different times during the week, with a midweek switch for two. It got to be more and more of a nightmare as this week approached. Still, I eventually found one friend whose daughter was a very good friend of my daughter, so they stayed together for that week. And I had a nephew who could never put up my daughter's braids, but he could certainly watch the two boys. So he sat at my house, and the kids all stayed within a block of each other.

This underlined something that I had been suspecting from the very first, that, yes, people offer help, but when the time actually comes, even with their good intentions, you are often on your own.

Next comes the last fallback—your place of work. Should you even try to take the kids along?

RD: Sometimes, if you have a decent employer and a really big emergency, you might be able to take a child to work with you. I try to do it as little as possible, and in some situations you can't do it at all. It helps to have understanding employers, and it helps to be open to your employers, letting them know that "This is the long-term situation I'm in. I have to take care of my kids on a regular basis. If there is an emergency for you and you need me, realize that I'm in this situation. And there may be an emergency for us in which I need your understanding."

If you've got a boss who doesn't understand this, you may have to start thinking about a different place of employment.

NB: When I was still in the navy, there were times when I did take my kids to work. You've got those midwatches; you've got to be there to relieve the watch. You pack everybody up, you bring a few toys or something and maybe some sleeping bags, and you find out which room they can sleep in.

Of course it's nice to let the shift supervisor know. And I found when I did bring the kids in, some people on the watch were somewhat disdainful, but they didn't say much about it. And you've got to really work at having the kids behave themselves. That's probably the worst part right there.

But there were times when some individuals on the watch didn't have much to do, so they actually helped out. They went and played with the kids for a while. They kept watch. They got a TV in there and did things like that.

And I've done it with a civilian employer, too. Sometimes you've got to take the kid to work, but you do want to make it a rarity. There was a time also when I was an employer, when I had a small business and somebody wanted to come to work for me. She said, "Well, sometimes I've got a little kid to take care of." So we made room and I told her to come on, bring him in. I told her, "Let's try not to interfere with what's going on with the job. You're here to work for me, not to watch your kid. But you've got to do both."

RD: I'd like to say I'm always understanding as a boss, and in my job at the newspaper I try very hard to be a sympathetic boss. But as a child-care customer I'm not so easy.

Part of it comes from my earliest decision that my kids shouldn't have to compromise in their own home. I realized that no matter how hard you try, children of a single parent are going to miss some-thing—immediate access to the other parent, more money in the home, certain activities, times when Mom and Dad both show up at the recital—something. So I swore that one thing they would not miss was the right to decide who would share their home. I would choose the child-care giver, but they would not be forced to live with sitters' kids, visiting friends, or sick spouses.

Part of that no-time-sharing decision comes from prior experi-ence: Before the divorce, we had a sitter who would arrive just before my then-wife, Toni, would head to work. Later, the sitter's boyfriend would drop off her youngest son, who was too young for school. By the afternoon, her three other kids would arrive from their schools—that made seven children and one adult in the house. One day the sitter's oldest son and mine decided to play gymnast on the closet coat rack. I still have a hole in the wall and no functioning coat rack.

NB: Of course in some cases where the person who is going to provide child care has children, you might want to consider taking your kids to their house and let them deal with the damage.

The combination of bosses and kids is such a potentially corrosive mixture, the media has coined a name for it—the mommy (or daddy) track. Is it possible to combine career and children and not get sidelined on the daddy track?

RD: Well, I have been—and I always tell people this—very lucky that the World's Greatest Newspaper seems to be comfortable with the needs and occasional emergencies that I've had to deal with: let-ting me split vacation weeks, letting me take time when I needed to, and not having it stand in the way of my progress through the organization.

The most recent promotion I got I was really afraid to apply for because it was only a year into the marital separation, and I didn't know if I could take on the extra responsibilities. That job, which I now have, was not just a promotion but also allowed me to go to grad school in an executive master's program, for which the *Chicago Tribune* paid most of the cost.

So I personally feel really lucky, but I do believe that the daddy track exists, just like the mommy track. Corporations set visible or invisible limits and, depending on where you are, they can be pretty strict as to how much your boss is going to accept.

Still, the one theme we seem to keep running up against in this discussion is that you've got to parent. There's no one else to watch the kids in these situations. Even if it's only for a day or a weekend, we are talking about situations where you can't rely on anyone else to take care of the kids. It's your responsibility, and it comes in front of responsibilities to work. That's my philosophy. And there may be no way to avoid being daddy-tracked. You may just have to accept it.

NB: I'm going to disagree with some of what you say on the daddy tracking. Whatever career you go into, there's going to be a limitation. It may be an educational background limitation; it may be a physical handicap limitation. But I'm sure there are still jobs that you can do.

I'm still working for the military, now the army, and right now I've got a pretty good deal where I can take time off when I need it. I have enough time in advance to plan my trips. I'm able to find someone to watch my daughter when I'm gone for several days. However, there are other jobs where you don't have that luxury, really, and it is kind of a luxury to have it.

But I think that for a lot of the daddy-tracking that you run into, the limitations are self-imposed. We're afraid to ask for help or understanding.

A lot of that self-imposition could easily be attributed to the fact that we're not very experienced as parents. It takes fifteen or twenty years to produce a reasonably experienced parent. And by that time most of the kids are gone and you're done with it. Do you really want to get into that again?

In my case, I've got the older boys who now are out on their own, but I've still got the one younger daughter, and it's almost like having two families. So I'm taking a lot of the lessons learned from the older boys, who, in retrospect, got the short end of the deal. Now their younger sister is benefiting from all the mistakes I made with them. I've been able to realize, "Well, if I could go back, I'd do it differently." I have the opportunity to do it differently and do it a little better here.

My Life as Solo Dad: Nick's Story

WE FELT THAT just as important as the lessons we are relating in this book are the life experiences we've had that led us to this book. So we'll take a break from the questions and answers here for a word from author Nick Borns.

When we were young and first married, as all young couples know, love conquers all. But after the years of the mental illness, as one thing after another was mounting up and working against us, there came a point in time where, despite how much I loved her, I had to make a decision that was best for the family, as difficult as it was. And, as an adult, I had to realize that love doesn't conquer all. It can go a long way, but even love has its limits.

The most obvious way to become a single parent is to have the other parent disappear from the scene through divorce or death. However, it is also possible to become a de facto single parent, even though you are still married and your partner is physically present. This was my path to single parenthood.

In late 1977 we lost our third child. Ilsa never made it out of the delivery room. We were overseas, isolated from both our families, and had relatively few friends at the time. But the command where I was serving was very supportive to both of us (at the time, I was in the navy and stationed on Guam). I took our daughter back to Arizona for burial in a family plot.

After I returned to Guam, things were not the same. The loss of a child is devastating to the best of marriages with both partners in good health. But throw in an unknown problem, like mental illness, and all bets are off.

About four years after we lost Ilsa, my wife's illness erupted with a vengeance. Patty was diagnosed with a schizoaffective disorder, an incurable mental illness, that can be treated with medication. We had some success with treatment while I was stationed in Monterey, California, and the future looked OK. Unfortunately, she would go off the medication and start another cycle of the illness. At first I didn't know why or when this would happen. Eventually I could roughly gauge the occurrence of the cycles but could not stop them.

I was transferred to a new command in Norfolk, Virginia, in 1983, and it was difficult to find the proper treatment. We had no friends or family to rely on. Patty went into the hospital with a relapse of her illness shortly after arriving in Norfolk. Over the next two years the hospitalizations became longer and more frequent. Financial strain resulted as the insurance was inadequate to deal with mental illness, and I had to find long-term child care, including overnight care. During the three years I was stationed at Norfolk, and for the year after I left the navy but still lived in the area, my wife was absent from the home nearly half the time, often for stretches of a month or longer. I was, in fact, raising the children on my own, even though my wife lived in the same house.

Becoming a single parent under these terms is, I believe, more difficult than going through divorce or the death of a spouse. For one thing, the other parent is still in the household and wants to retain authority as a parent, even though she or he is not capable of doing so. And there is very little support for parents in such situations. Several people, including a navy chaplain and our pediatrician, advised me to seek a divorce and take care of the children myself. But the thought of divorce was repugnant to me. I had been taught that it was not an acceptable choice.

Instead I sought help from our respective families. My wife needed to concentrate on treating her illness, at least to the point where she would be able to function, even in a limited capacity. The health-care professionals overseeing her treatment gave little heed to my concerns. As I explained that the stress in the family was too much for her to handle and suggested halfway houses or group homes as more beneficial than hospitalization, I was told such things either did not exist or were not available in her case.

I had a little better luck with her family as far as having her return home to be treated. Unfortunately, her mother and younger sister, also living at home, suffered from similar mental illnesses.

I suddenly found myself faced with a new set of challenges and consequences. Changes were coming in work, home life, social life, and some areas never thought about before. I was not expecting most of the changes, although I knew there would be some. Early in the transition I expected that there would be a way for things to function normally, although the truth was that there would be a new definition of normal.

The cycles of Patty's illness had a dramatic effect on my job in 1983. At that point in my navy career I needed to go to sea. However, due to my wife's mental illness, I was forced to cancel the orders and stay ashore instead. This was a major strike against my chances to get promoted and finish a naval career.

(I should note that my brother in Tucson had offered to have my family stay with him while I went to sea. However, the thought of my family in Arizona when I was home-ported out of Norfolk did not sit well. It meant that I would miss about two and a half years of my children's lives. This was not a reasonable prospect for me at that time. In retrospect I still wonder if I made the correct decision.)

Next, the extra duties as a single parent needing child care for three—and, later, four—children presented some major obstacles. I worked a rotating, twelve-hour shift, and finding consistent child care was difficult at best. There were more and more times when I would be late for work because I had to wait for the sitter to come or had to get everyone packed up and dropped off at a sitter's home. It soon became obvious that I had not chosen a very good place to live, since I had a thirty-five-minute commute and was separated from the navy community. On or near the base I could have found adequate care more easily. Also, I would have been in a community that would have understood my work needs better.

The area where I lived, in Chesapeake, Virginia, had a primarily civilian population. The neighbors tended to keep to themselves. None of them knew me very well, and with all the needs of my family, few wanted to be close enough to be counted on. Certainly they were cordial and helped out in small ways. But I found myself stuck in the house, working or running errands, so that I seldom had the opportunity to cultivate any meaningful friendships in the neighborhood.

The next impact on my job was less direct. Since I spent so much more time taking care of family, my marks on fitness reports started slipping. I did not participate in as many voluntary activities as other officers and spent less extra time at the command doing additional duty. This had the effect of reducing my competitiveness with fellow officers when it came time for promotion.

Ultimately, without sea duty and with slightly lowering marks, I was passed over twice for promotion and was forced off active duty in 1986.

With more than eleven years of service to that time, I opted to join the naval reserve and hoped to be able to put in the remaining nine years to qualify for a reserve retirement and not lose the previous years of effort toward that goal.

The few friends we had were married and maintained more normal social lives. I soon found us invited to few, and then none, of the social functions normally associated with friends. There were no invitations to dinner or to share an outing with the family. Invitations to visit our house always seemed to be made at the wrong time. Eventually the social isolation was nearly complete. I associated with colleagues only at work.

I knew I needed to keep some semblance of normalcy, not just for the children's well-being but for my own as well. But I had few outlets to distract me from the daily grind. I found it was necessary to really work at keeping things going on a daily basis to avoid a major bout of depression.

This was another aspect I had not anticipated or expected—personal depression. The incidents of isolation that occurred over the years had mounted. They tended to be cumulative, so it was not always noticeable in day-to-day life.

For much of my early time as a solo dad, a major question was whether to act as a single parent or try to include my wife, who was less and less involved in running the household. Circumstance and time began to force the issue. The children needed to have a stable environment on which to base their values.

Within a few years I had become a single parent with an occasional visit from the other parent. This actually made life a bit simpler, and it seemed to put the children more at ease. I had now become the single parental authority in the house. My wife exercised parental authority only through my support.

And this had another negative side. Conflict over what actions should be taken for the children was more damaging to Patty if she chose to raise this conflict in front of them. And more and more often, an argument happened in front of them and I was forced to overrule her. Since I was the only consistent parent, it was necessary for me to retain the authority. But she seemed to choose to challenge me rather than talk in private. I found myself becoming dictatorial in our relationship, and this created a greater rift between us. As Patty's illness progressed, I chose to deal less with her illness and put more emphasis on maintaining as much stability for the children as possible.

Also, the symptoms of her illness were considerable: manic and depressive periods that would range from sullenness to out-of-control joy, mood swings of huge intensity in the space of a short conversation, and vocal outbursts that later turned to physical violence against inanimate objects or, rarely, people.

After the death of our third son, Stephen, who was killed in a traffic accident in 1985, there was less and less communication between Patty and me. I became more and more irritated by her apparent refusal to stay on her medication and adequately treat her illness, and I began to spend more and more time with the children. My anger overtook my love for her. I believed that if it was not important to her to treat her illness effectively, why should I be concerned with how well she was?

By the spring of 1986 it was apparent that my naval career would end soon and I would have to find other employment. This meant looking at my skills and how best to sell them to a new employer. I had not gotten any advanced degrees during my time in the navy, mainly due to the nature of my duty assignments. So I started graduate school, taking one or two classes each semester at first, then trying to expand to more so that I could finish the degree (a master of arts in international studies) before my education benefits under the Vietnam-era GI Bill ran out. Unfortunately, due to changes made by the U.S. Congress, the money was running out faster than I anticipated. Eventually, I was forced by economics to stop this degree effort and look at other options.

In the spring of 1987, I applied to Indiana University in Bloomington. My house was up for sale, and it looked as though all would turn out all right. I assumed the lower cost of living in Indiana, as well as being closer to family, would be better for us, plus I could get a master's and improve my employability.

Due to my military status, I was still considered a resident of Indiana. In July 1987, I was accepted at IU's graduate school in geography. I began to make arrangements to move to Bloomington. Of course, I was still actively seeking permanent employment, especially in the government sector. Unfortunately, success in this arena was not to be found.

I sent out résumés to any company I could find that might use my skills as a meteorologist or to which I could adapt. I went on quite a few interviews, some requiring overnight drives. Job hunting proved to be quite frustrating, especially since I had not had to look for a job for a decade. It had been my intention to finish a military career with at least twenty years of service (and I did remain in the naval reserve for the next ten years to qualify for a reserve retirement). In the short term the additional pay I received from extra reserve activity did a great deal to help make ends meet. Though there were many times when the future looked quite bleak, I always believed that God would provide an opportunity for me. Meanwhile, I just had to keep looking.

Also in spring 1987, it became obvious that the house in Chesapeake was too expensive to maintain. Selling the house produced some interesting situations. Patty did not want to sell, even though I explained to her that it was financially impossible for us to stay. On several occasions after a prospective client had looked at the house, she came outside and announced the house was not for sale and that the client should leave immediately. This did chase away some potential buyers.

Preparing to ship the household goods was also a challenge. The navy owed me one last move, and I fully intended to take them up on it. I arranged for the movers' agent to visit the house to determine how much would be involved in the move. But once when I was out of town on an interview, Patty refused to let the agent into the house, stating that we were not moving. Eventually it was necessary to arrange a "do-it-yourself" move.

The summer of 1987 proved to be quite eventful, to say the least. It became the year that I lost custody of my kids.

I had taken the children with me to Bloomington on a househunting trip when I went to register for the fall semester. I still went on job interviews, and my wife still was absent, even when she was physically present. Yet I had to rely on my wife's presence to handle things at home so that I could take care of the move and keep money coming in. Our relationship rapidly deteriorated during that summer. She refused to understand the need to move.

As a result, there were increasing arguments between us. Also, some of the neighbors began making complaints to the Chesapeake Child Protective Service (CPS).

The intervention of the CPS quickly complicated matters. For one thing, CPS decided to maintain jurisdiction by hindering any move out of town, not to mention out of state.

At first there was support from my wife's family. However, after Patty spent the night in the county jail on a contempt-of-court charge, I lost that support. I chose to let her stay in jail once I learned at the lockup that I would have to drag three children through three hours of legal proceedings, starting at about 11:00 P.M., to bail her out. Furthermore, I would be responsible to get her to a court hearing. Since the contempt charge stemmed from her leaving the court before a scheduled child-welfare hearing could be held, I knew that I could not guarantee such action. But I was never able to convince her family that I had done the right thing.

The CPS moved very quickly after that, and the children were put into foster care at my expense. At this time, there was no divorce or separation action pending or even discussed.

Late in 1987, I received a job offer from the National Weather Service in Maine. My financial and family situations were intolerable and made it impossible for me to pursue grad school in Indiana, so I accepted the job. But now I had to move my household goods from Bloomington, Indiana, to Caribou, Maine. Upon arrival in Caribou in January 1988, I had to make preparations for the family to move there. The CPS conditions were that I would have to establish a household and have child care arranged before the court would allow the children to move with me. In the meantime, they were transferred to their grandparents in Valparaiso, Indiana, for indefinite residence. I wound up going to Maine by myself.

At this point I decided that trying to keep the marriage together was a lost cause. I found this quite sad, yet my only recourse was to establish a household as quickly as possible so that the children would be able to join me. I found myself having to travel around the county looking for a place to live and set up house.

I have never been an extrovert. I normally stay within my very local world of family, school, and work to build my social contacts. Fortunately, my co-workers at Caribou were all good people. They began to include me in their schedules, which went a long way toward taking the edge off the isolation. Also, I found the people in Caribou and much of Aroostook County to be quite friendly. It made for a good quality of life, and I was able to become more "extroverted." I began to make contacts more quickly with regard to child care, housing, schools, and social opportunities in the area.

Living in Caribou was one of the highlights of my time as a single parent. The preparations I needed to complete forced me to look at the family situation from a new perspective. I knew success in reuniting the family would come chiefly from my efforts. I had to accept that I could no longer rely on others to take care of the home front.

I did not date anyone while in Maine, since I was still married, but I did work at developing other social contacts. I finally started doing some things that I had only dreamed or talked about. I went to the library regularly. I socialized with co-workers. I learned to cross-country ski—perhaps my most enjoyable endeavor.

Even though I skied by myself, I found it quite exhilarating and relaxing. I would take a tape player and headset and listen to some of my favorite music. Skiing allowed me to think of quite a few things: fun, serious, fantastic, as well as nothing at all. Just being in the stillness of a wilderness area was quite enjoyable. It was during skiing that I made the conscious decision to take a job that the U.S. Army had offered me.

After about two months at Caribou, the army sent a letter offering me a position in Madison, Indiana, if they could get around a hiring freeze. Two months after that, late on a Thursday, they called and said they wanted me to report to work the next Monday. It took a while, but I was able to convince them that Indiana was not next door to Maine and that I would also have to give reasonable notice to the weather service before leaving.

Moving to Indiana in May 1988 put me much closer to the children. However, I would have to start over with the preparations that I had all but completed in Caribou. Again, there were no friends or family in the immediate vicinity, although one of my sisters was now only three-hundred miles away. I was still in legal battles with CPS, but I was able to establish a proper household.

I was also fortunate to be dealing with a child welfare agency that I believe actually put the welfare of the children first. The case-workers in Indiana were very matter-of-fact and diligent in their jobs. The caseworker in Valparaiso, where the children were with their grandparents, eventually strongly recommended that the kids be returned home to me. And the caseworker in Madison kept very close tabs on what I was doing and gave very specific guidance on what I needed to do.

The only fly in the ointment showed up when Patty came down to Madison. She called the caseworker and introduced herself. After one long meeting, the caseworker let me know in no uncertain terms that if Patty were to remain in the household, the caseworker would deem it unfit for the children. Shortly thereafter, I filed for a legal separation. At this point in 1988, Karl was twelve, Nick was eleven, and Christina was three and a half.

I tried to explain to Patty that this was intended as a temporary arrangement, that she needed to get treatment that was not available at the time in Madison, but which she was already getting in Valparaiso. I told her that I would take care of the children and the house and she would take care of herself. Once she progressed sufficiently in her treatment, she could return and we could have a united family again. But she refused to accept this as likely, and her family immediately began legal maneuvers designed to delay a decision. However, I did get the children returned to me on a permanent basis.

The next two years were a combination of legal struggles as the separation progressed to divorce, a rushed effort to complete a master's degree (this time in education) before my military educational benefits ran out, work at my regular job, and the naval reserve. The legal battles with my in-laws did nothing to help their daughter's mental state, and I soon wiped all hope of reconciliation from my mind and did my best to make a clean break from the marriage.

As a family unit the children and I eventually functioned fairly well. They were quite happy to return after nearly a year away. Chores were designated and sometimes even done. The main sign of effects from the separation came when it was time for them to visit their mother. They wouldn't cooperate: "I'm not going to pick up. I'm not going to pack. Why do I have to go? Why can't I stay with friends?" It was an argument rebellion.

By 1991, life in Madison began to settle down to some sort of routine. I had nearly finished my degree. The divorce was final, and I had gotten an extra vehicle, an old van from the army. I focused my efforts on learning how to deal with two teenage boys and one little girl fast growing into a rambunctious child.

The older boys helped immensely with baby-sitting, and I had become friendly with the neighbors across the street who had children slightly older than my oldest. This allowed me to go on my two-week naval reserve trips, which were financially quite important: my income from the reserve paid the mortgage. It took quite a bit of doing to work full-time and then also go on the reserve trips, but it was worth it in the long run.

Still, southern Indiana was not Caribou, Maine. It was more difficult for me to get into any social activities outside of work. The people were friendly but tended to keep to themselves. As a newcomer, I was pretty much out of any social circles, unless they were of people who were also not native to the area.

The children's visits with their mother in northern Indiana were quite difficult at first but eased over time. My daughter was required to visit every month, but the boys were only to come up every other month. The trips were stressful for everyone.

The lack of any personal relationship added to the stress. I made a conscious effort not to discuss the marital situation with any of the children, but I was not always successful. Long-distance phone calls to my sister helped a lot, but once the phone was hung up, the vacuum from the absence of another adult was still there. Over time, even the most common tasks began to become more laborious than they really were.

Not having someone to share with, to confide in, just to be in the vicinity of, slowly added to the stress of everyday life. I began to become preoccupied with finding someone or something to fill this void.

I opted to start a small business. I thought that a part-time activity like this would allow me to meet other people, bring in a little extra cash, and provide good business experience for the boys as well as put some spending money in their pockets. This last reason sounded even better when the boys, now fifteen and sixteen, found it hard to find jobs in town. Since I couldn't help out with any contacts in the community, it seemed reasonable to me to create a job for my boys, possibly even a decent business when they graduated from high school.

Unfortunately, my zeal for a business exceeded my ability to make things happen in an efficient manner. Rather than providing a common activity for the whole family with reasonable benefits, the business became a lodestone. Tempers raged, nerves were frayed, sleep lost. True, it did provide money to the boys, but at an hourly wage much below the minimum wage they could have gotten at a burger joint.

I believed that perseverance would pay off, but I was wrong. I became obsessed with trying to make the business work. We did have some successes in the third year, but by then the boys were graduating from high school and needed a more substantial future.

I was now faced with new problems and challenges. How do I get my children through college? At about this point I lost sight of one of my major responsibilities and confused it with my own dreams. I chose to pursue the business and try to make it work with only part-time help.

To add fuel to this fire, the military base where I was working was to be closed by September 1995. I had hoped to make the business more profitable so as to stay in Madison, but the choices I faced were to find a job locally or find another job in army civil service. Another army job meant moving again. This meant once again losing my support network. I would be moving farther away, probably out of state. This would also have an impact on visitation for the kids.

I decided to do my best to make the business work. I opted to open a small winery. The good part was that wineries in Indiana are a growth industry. Unfortunately, I did not have a secure supply of grapes or the resources to get it started right. I did find ways to start production and sales, right during one of the worst fall and winter seasons for tourist businesses in Madison. Despite producing reasonably good wines that were enjoyed by most who stopped in, there just weren't enough sales to cover operations.

I finally came to my senses and took the transfer with the army and moved to Maryland. Moving to Maryland was a mixed bag. The older boys were now on their own, leaving only my daughter at home. Because the move came in September, early in the school year, I opted to leave Christina in Madison with friends until I was able to find a permanent place to live.

The business had left my finances in a shambles, but I was able to find a reasonable option. I eventually bought a HUD property that needed lots of repair, but the price was far below market value.

I also found the social outlook much more promising. After a few months of sitting alone in my apartment, I discovered Parents Without Partners. I attended one of their membership meetings and then joined. I soon found myself meeting many other single parents. I was anxious for a new and closer relationship than I had had for the first years after my divorce. I soon met someone with whom I would become very close for the next year and more.

As soon as school was out in Madison, I got Christina and brought her to her new home. She was sad, of course, to leave her friends; I would have stayed in Indiana if there had been any way for me to make a living. But in late summer, an Irish dance group started up, and my daughter joined. She made some very good friends very quickly, and it helped her adjustment to be a part of a group like this.

I had to drive her twenty miles for the group meetings, and, since it was too far a distance to drop her off and then go home, it also opened up new opportunities for me to meet with the other parents.

Once the house got into livable condition, we worked on unpacking household goods and just settling in. Our family situation has changed significantly. With the two older boys out on their own, I now have an "only child" situation, and can do more things with my daughter as she enters her teen years than I did with my sons.

She is also more independent and capable than many other children her age, which I am sure is due to her home life. She has had to do more for herself, such as cleaning her room, doing laundry and yardwork, cooking, and other chores. She has also helped in our family business since she was six. I often find myself teaching her business principles and helping her exercise her entrepreneurial skills.

But being the single parent of an only child brings up other issues, both with my daughter and with my partner and her own children. I don't know all the answers, but I am working on it.

Being a single parent is a really tough job. Being a single, custodial father makes it a little tougher. Our society does not prepare men for parenting, let alone single parenting. Even in this enlightened age of equality, men are still expected to be breadwinners and women caretakers of the home and children. I feel fortunate that my parents, especially my mother, provided examples of how to take care of children. I only hope that I can pass on some of my experience to other men who are faced with being solo dads.

Part II

Taking Care of Mom

WE KNEW THIS section would have to be included for every solo dad, because whether you are going solo for the afternoon or solo through a few childhoods, Mom's presence is always there. Whether she is shopping, divorced, ill, or deceased, she is mixed into nearly every action and all encounters you and your children have.

No surprise here—the biological, psychological, sociological, and psychic bonds of mother and child are indisputable, and even in those situations where there is no true bond (such as through a mother's death during her child's infancy, or severe family dysfunction), society tells us there must be a bond, or at least an emptiness where that bond should be. The legal systems of nations, the religions, social welfare systems, cultural mores—almost all have a definition of mother-child relations, even where father-child relations may not be so clearly defined.

The psychic umbilical cord is never truly cut.

Dealing with this truth, however, was not so easily accomplished. There are so many variations on the theme of why Dad has the kids now, it is very hard to supply general guidelines or discuss situations that have much breadth without being obscure, vague, or boringly predictable.

However, we followed the solo dad's creed to soldier on as best we could. We stuck closely to the pattern of relating our individual experiences with our kids, ourselves, and our emotions, and we hope that they will provide some directions to go in, if not instructions to follow, for each solo dad struggling with the question of "Where is Mom?"

The Case of the Missing Mom

ONE OF THE first lessons we learn as infants is that things go away. Sometimes things go out of our field of vision, like those little hands we are trying so hard to control. Sometimes we can make things go, and they come back, like the toy we just threw out of the crib for the fourteenth time. And sometimes things go and never come back. Then we learn about longing.

Absence and longing are naturally occurring events in life, but when they are linked to permanent loss, to divorce, death, or illness, keeping them in perspective becomes much more difficult. Even a simple trip by one parent to the grocery store can be a stress-filled hour for the other parent and the kids if that remaining parent is wrapped up in anger or fear.

So if the first step for solo dads is to keep your feelings of longing and absence in the perspective of life, the second is to remember that feelings are allowable and expected. You can feel angry when abandoned, and hurt and grieving at a loss, especially in front of children. It is necessary for children to see that their parents have emotions, even though this is not the easiest thing for a man to demonstrate. You can cry in front of them and with them, you can show your anger, sorrow, and longing, and you really should. Just make sure you explain that Dad feels these emotions and why Dad feels them. Reassure your children that they are not responsible for rattling Dad's emotions or for soothing them but that they can share their emotions with you. And help them learn what you will do to survive the wave of emotions, whether that will be to ride the tide, to seek assistance, to cry or shout, or to hug them a little longer. Expressing emotions is key.

And expressing them honestly is the color of the key. Don't worry about being polite about loss or covering up the facts. If Mom left us for a new life, we as dads have the right to say that and to say that we are angry about it. As one psychiatric counselor said, you should not let the other partner determine alone what the child sees as your adult relationship. Just don't turn your kids into a court panel—let them know that you see things differently and you remember events another way and that they will have plenty of time to decide what they feel about everything that has happened. They don't have to decide who is right or wrong, they just need to know that they can have feelings about Mom and Dad and those feelings can change.

But even brief absences can give rise to emotional quandaries, and the authors are advocates of continued, if not full, disclosure. It will probably do no good to say, "Junior, Mom left for a shopping spree and Dad couldn't find the stove if he tripped over it and broke his nose. If she doesn't come home soon, we'll all starve. Now go and play."

But you can be at a loss about what to do for dinner, how to pass the time, or whether to kiss that boo-boo or call the paramedics. It's OK to say, "I'm nervous because I don't know what to do about this. I'm a beginner." (Then you send the kid off to get this book from the bookshelf, and you read about what Nick and Reg did.)

Dealing with the unasked question "Where's Mom?" can be a lot more serious. A wide variety of guilt, anger, and fear can keep kids from asking this question. Though there are generalizations to be made, each child responds in his or her individual way, just as each adult does. But, because the question is so important to all of us, each child does respond.

RD: One general comment, which I heard from a televised therapist, is that up through the age of eight children use "magical reasoning." They think that, no matter what, their personal magic caused an event to happen. If it was a bad event, they caused it to happen because they were bad, and if only they could be very, very good, they could somehow change the event or make it "unhappen."

I find this to be a very significant lesson, but I have three children who were eight or younger when my marriage went south, and each one of them has a completely different way of expressing what he or she feels. Andi had, and still has, bouts of acting out, refusing to do daily routines and then coming to screams and tears. Paul will brood a while, then ask a serious question or two that goes to the heart of the matter. And Mike is my vacuum bottler. He should carry a warning label: "Contents under pressure." He takes his emotions and swallows them, and I still haven't found any way to get those thoughts and feelings out. I am certain his problems in school—not sticking to task, not finishing homework or not turning it in, inability to talk to his teachers—stem from this emotional magma building up in him.

But it's much different from living with a volcano, because this volcano is my own little boy, and I know the forthcoming explosion is going to hurt him as well as his mother and me. And I still don't know how to relieve the pressure.

Nick's experience was more unusual, because he had to tell children about an illness that did not show symptoms of fever or sneezes but was even more serious.

NB: When they were younger, they were asking about their mom's illness. All I could really tell them was that Mom was sick, she had an illness and that was the plain truth of it, and it was an illness that was not curable, but it was treatable. And there was some concern from them: "Why? What's going on here?"

RD: Did you find, or can you recall now thinking back, signs, behavior—things that are not so direct as asking "Where is Mom?" Did you have situations where the behavior was not a direct sign of the problem but let you know there was a problem?

NB: Oh, sometimes they could be extremely indirect about things. They all acted differently, because they were different ages when significant events happened. Christina has not had too much trouble with it because she was so young when everything started. Actually, she wasn't born. So she's grown up with this as the way things are. Karl was more straightforward, although he would hold things in a lot, like I do sometimes. Nick was more reactive, and a couple of times he ran away from home. But we usually found him hiding somewhere just outside the house.

And while we were in Madison, Indiana, and he was in his midteens, Nick got very defensive about his mother. Karl was very direct: he didn't want to go up and see her; he didn't want to deal with it. And that started a rift between the two of them. I tried to keep them calmed down, saying, "You each should deal with your mother the way you need to. Don't fight each other about it." Nick just took it a little more to heart, and that caused some problems between us. Probably for a while he blamed me for how she was.

RD: Just recently, Paul showed me signs of his strong feelings about his mother.

Paul hates to have anybody tease him with nicknames. So I called home one day after he had gotten home from school, and he blurted out, "I had a horrible day. A terrible day." I asked what had happened, and he said, "I got into a fight with two of the boys in my class." This was highly unusual for Paul—like most "babies of the family," he's learned it's much more profitable to tattle to adults than to take direct physical action. (At least that's the way I learned it.)

Beyond these first statements, he wouldn't really tell me what the fight was about. He just said it was because they called him names. They called my far-too-handsome son "ugly."

By the time I got home, he was really upset. He couldn't do his homework; he would suddenly burst into tears. Every time I'd hug him, talk to him, and get him settled down and back to task, he would just cry and cry and cry. Finally I said, "Do you want me to talk to your mother?" He said, quite emotionally, "No, I don't want you to call Mom." But I convinced myself that I was going to have to call her just to get him some mommy comfort. I felt that there was something here that was not coming out to me, but maybe it would come out to her. Just as I was phoning her, Michael came downstairs and said, "I found out what really happened." The boys had told Paul a "yo mama's so fat" joke. It was truly unfunny insult humor, and what's more, it was exceptionally inaccurate. Anybody who has ever seen Toni knows that Toni has never been fat.

I realized that this joke had nothing to do with reality, but because they said something mean about his mother, it had made Paul more angry than I have ever seen him. He threw things at one child and even refused to apologize. And once I talked to him about the whole incident, he cried again, but he was able to calm down. So I can understand what you mean about one child becoming defensive about his mother.

Another issue in dealing with Mom is handling the hand-off. Even the simplest exchange of children between parents can become an incident for tears and tantrums. The most common time for problems is in infant and toddler years, because the child may have a definite preference for one parent, usually caregiver-and-feeder Mom. But these cases are handled easily with a quick movement away from the other parent, some soothing words and hugs, and, perhaps, the appeasement of a toy or pacifier.

What may occur as children get older are instances when they act to subvert the planned exchange, refusing to get ready, putting off a necessary task, or forgetting it. The signs of distress are obvious, and using normal dad discipline—"Just do it! Now!"—does not get to the issue: why the child does not want to go.

RD: On occasion, Paul wouldn't want to go to his mom's house, and I had tremendous emotional problems dealing with it. I knew that by their visiting Mom, I was going to get a little bit of solitude, and I had a motivation to encourage visits. No matter how much you love anybody, sometimes you need a little time alone. Another part, a second third of my thoughts on this, told me that she had a right to see them and she did love them. I shouldn't encourage him to stay away from his mom, because it would hurt him at least as much as it would hurt her. But the third third of me was saying I should not force this child to go.

So, each time his reluctance showed up, we'd sit down, the two of us and sometimes the three of us, with Toni. We would talk, and I would say, "I'm not going to force you, but why don't you want to go?" And almost always the reason was that he wanted to play the video game. Well, I don't think a video game is an acceptable excuse for not seeing your parent, so we would talk some more and much of his reluctance would fade and he would go.

Still, I am afraid that some of that reluctance was his way of dealing with the divorce. The more I replay those conversations, the more I feel that he is uncomfortable with switching from one house to another. I have seen absolutely nothing wrong with his mom's boyfriend. He seems to be fine with them and with his own daughter, and I get no complaints of how he treats them. But Paul is no fan of new things or strangers, and it's taken him a long time to get comfortable with any new adult.

The handoff for visitation during forced separations, such as divorce, can cause emotional problems for fathers as well. Divorce almost always leaves behind feelings of rejection and resentment, and this is one time when emotions are not useful. There is too much potential damage to the children when parents start swinging those verbal axes they've been grinding through the week.

RD: My advice, at least at the first few times for the handoff, would be to try to drain as much emotion as you can out of the event. Be cordial, reconfirm the pickup time, try not to get into discussions of anything serious, and try very hard not to get a fight started. I think I started out poorly, often putting on an attitude as if I had cause to be miffed or she had shown some sign that she didn't believe I had cause. But she was smart enough that she never rose to the bait. Maybe she didn't even recognize my 'tude.

I've now gotten to the point where I have respect for her boyfriend, I understand her new life. We talk about news, school, work, family. She'll tell me a bit about her health; I'll chat about mine. We could almost be friends. We never get to a too-sympathetic position. The time for that is gone, but we do exchange personal information and don't feel uncomfortable.

Part of my problem early on came from people advising me with a long list of *shouldn'ts*: "Your ex-wife shouldn't come into your house; she should wait outside. She shouldn't change plans unexpectedly, and if she's not there on time, you should leave. You shouldn't go to her house to pick up the children; she should bring them back." All these demands that I was supposed to make.

The thought of keeping track of those demands, and declaring and enforcing them, really upset me. I found the best thing to do was to get rid of those rules. If she's supposed to see them today and if she is over a half hour late, yeah, then we might go out somewhere. But if we didn't have plans to go out or we don't seem upset about staying home, we don't leave just to spite her. If she calls to say she's running late, then we can wait. She comes inside and helps them gather things to take with them on the trip. If I need to go pick them up, I pick them up.

It's more important to me that I have them. It's more important to me that she and I relate peaceably and that the kids see we relate peaceably. It's more important that we are all comfortable in our lives than that I have to push everybody through all these hoops.

NB: When I was taking them up to Valparaiso, Indiana, sometimes it would be very easy, and sometimes it would get very tough. Patty would want to talk about something, and that was a very dangerous thing for me to do, but I didn't want to just slam the door and run out either. So I would try to talk. As long as she kept it regarding the kids, that was fine. But sometimes she'd want to move it back to why she couldn't come up with me over the navy reserve weekend and let the kids stay with Grandma and Grandpa. I would tell her, "No, we can't do that. I'm working." And sometimes she would get upset about it.

And here appears the other side to that emotional pendulum: having to deal with your feelings that are still there for someone you once pledged your life to.

NB: Yes, there are still feelings there. I've had my twinges, even in the last couple of years, that maybe we could think about rebuilding something. We were married for a long time. It didn't start for no reason. And, at least with me, emotions die hard.

I'd get to thinking about that, and I'd be talking to her, and she'd get to saying some things, and then I'd snap to—"OK, I need a reality check"—and my mind would click on the tape of why we got divorced in the first place.

I went to a Parents Without Partners meeting a while back, and there was a lawyer talking about divorce. She made the comment that at some point the divorce is final. The judge says it's final; all right, it's over. All I could think of was that she was new at this.

Yes, the marriage is over, and I emphasize that the marriage is over because that's a legal state. But in this situation where children are involved, the relationship is far from over. Only the marriage is over. You've still got to deal with that relationship. And I was thinking, "This lawyer is telling people it's over; the storm has passed. Everything is going to be coming up roses." Not quite. There's a lot of fertilizer coming up on those roses first. And you're going to have to deal with that stuff every day.

You need to remember why you got divorced. Sometimes you have to remind yourself of that, because you get lonely and you start wondering if maybe this split was not a good idea. You need to remind yourself that you got divorced and there were very good reasons for it.

RD: There is the possibility that you are trying to fall back into something that you feel is easy. It's easier to return to a bad relationship than to give up on it and find another. I've got children with this person. It seems easier to go back and try to pick up that relationship than to go through the whole meeting-dating-talking-and-all-that-other process. It may seem easy in the short run, but it can be even more devastating over a slightly longer term. Suddenly I'm back with this person I couldn't trust or couldn't live with before.

My experience has been, and maybe I don't know what love is, but this is the only woman I have ever really loved. There are still very strong emotions. But one thing that kept me from trying it again with her was that she always had someone else.

I actually work at making sure I do not get too involved when she's feeling sick or when she's tired or if she's having emotional problems. But there are still feelings there. It took me a long time to find somebody in my life: I was twenty-eight when I got married. And it's five years out of the marriage, and I'm barely dating. It took me a long time to make that emotional attachment, and it is going to take me a long time to let go. I'm kind of lucky in that she has never been alone. That was my reminder of why we got divorced.

NB: I just wanted to point out that even at our "advanced age" hormones are still playing hell with us, and they are going to interfere with what logic tells us.

Desmond Morris, in his TV series "The Human Animal," really struck the point home about why are we doing this. There are chemicals in our bodies that set things off. And these hormones, even at forty and fifty, are still setting things off. I now have a better understanding of why this is happening. So I say I had better satisfy my hormonal needs elsewhere before I get into a situation with my former wife where I can't handle it.

I still can't deal with taking care of her mental illness. Whatever happens, it's beyond my ability to fix it or even try to be the good Martian who listens to the Venusian. But I am glad that I understand that Mars-Venus analogy better. It has helped. I will sit there and listen to her talk and give a sympathetic ear sometimes, but I don't let it go to my head and think she's made progress and so maybe we can do something here.

Our relationship on that level is done and is never going to be rekindled. I've been able to force myself to realize that, and I hope other divorced people will realize that for themselves. If they can, they can probably have a better divorce relationship than they did a marriage relationship. If not, they won't be able to handle the handoffs with the kids, or the other times when they have to deal with the ex, without the danger of getting romantically involved again or getting angry for the wrong reasons.

My Life as Solo Dad: Reg's Story

HERE'S THE SECOND half of our solo dad personal testimony. Relating his life experiences over the last five years as a single parent is Reg Davis.

There is a gain that comes out of loss, a lesson and a comfort and a shaft of strength that braces you. It comes from having survived and then moving on. It's more than the lesson of the blues; it's a jazz tune that takes sorrow and survival and pushes on toward discovery and exaltation. I no doubt will hit some blue notes in this solo, but the exaltation is coming. I'll even start off with a preview:

There is no more profound evolution, no greater calling, and no more marvelous development for a man than to become a true father to children. Unfortunately, these modern times require that I add the qualifier *true*. This is to distinguish fathering from fatherhood and raising children from siring them. But, if what I see is true, we modern men are also changing the verb *father* to mean "nurture, enhance, motivate, love, and support young life." It is a wonderful job, providing continually renewable pleasure in the way good food and good sex are renewable. It is a joy to father.

I often feel I'm much more of a defender than a practitioner of love. I thought I had married, helped form a family, worked and learned and progressed (and cursed and struggled and failed) out of love for all. Now I'm not so sure it was love at all, especially when things can't and don't and won't work out. But I believe in love and in loving your kids most of all.

The breakup of my marriage was common enough to be photocopied out of any of a thousand personal biographies. These are the most distinctive details of the mess that finally collapsed of its own weight:

On May 13, two days after our thirteenth wedding anniversary, we had what became our last session with the marriage counselor. I walked in feeling unwanted, used for some purpose none of us really understood. I had tried to talk to my wife, Toni, about how I felt, and she had told me. "Tell the counselor. What do you want me to say, that it's going to be all right? It's not going to be all right." A day or so after that conversation, and a few days before the counseling session, we went out for an anniversary dinner. It was worse than a first date. I had to consider this disaffection and lack of communication, along with months of financial crisis, evenings alone, and a holiday when she never came home. Putting all of that together, it was more than I wanted to continue.

"I want it over," I said in the counseling session. "I want her out, or me out, but I want it to end." And, with surprisingly little argument and some tears, the marriage was done.

That sounds too simple. In real time it was more than a year later that it was legally done: divorce papers signed, alimony and cash payments and college bills agreed to. And, though all hopes of maintaining the marriage ended that morning hour in a small office in a suburban Chicago building in May 1993, the marriage itself had died a few years before.

The toxins that had killed the marriage were household and mundane. Two people growing apart. Too much career, too much isolation, not enough attention. One person seeking what the other could never give; the other person expecting to get what the first never had. Having three children did not bring on the problems, nor did their presence stop the decay. There was coldness and withdrawal. There were lies. There was infidelity.

I don't think that identifying which party took what action carries much importance. We each allowed a promising love to fade and die; neither of us could save a relationship that had its troubles from the start.

So on May 13, 1993, we began the process of separating the household. And, in fits and starts, we each also began the process of becoming a single parent.

This book already tells the story of my first realization of what it meant to be a single father—a vaudeville act of juggling career, kids, and all the household duties without even the illusion of a partner to catch a few responsibilities on their way down. But that first year was full of cruel discoveries and anger and attempts at retribution. Friends finally felt they could come forward with witnessed accounts that confirmed what was already known about our dying marriage. First statements we filed with the court made each of us look like a Dickensian monster. She moved out of state to her mother's house; I refused to send her money. Visitation was infrequent and awkward, and I developed an (unfounded) fear that Toni would try to abduct the children from me. At one point she filed for custody of the children and the marital home. I filed for sole custody. We could not cooperate.

I thank God and "Mother (*Chicago*) *Tribune*" for understanding bosses, because in many ways I was a wreck. Household duties, school responsibilities, and my own mental health squeezed in on what effort I could put into work. Yet, even with all their understanding, there was a job promotion I had wanted and didn't get. For all the right reasons that I could see for not getting it, what hurt most was knowing that, even if I had gotten the job, I would have had no time to do it properly.

At home I used various friends, relatives, and baby-sitters to fill in the time I couldn't give myself, but I tried to give much more than was possible. My finances were a shambles, so I pinched pennies and shopped sales and worried about dressing the kids. The pleasure I used to get from buying little extravagances had to turn to enjoyment from just being able to buy groceries that week. And finding time to do things was the only goal of this hunter-gatherer. Forget books— I barely had time to read the paper, and that was part of my job.

I had lost my stepfather in November of 1992, and later in 1993 both my father and my one remaining grandparent, his mother, died. My mother had died of cancer just before Toni and I began dating, and I felt more and more alone.

At the same time, the kids were trying to deal with school, their own growth, and this sudden split in their family, and they suffered. Michael played the stoic big brother, and his efforts in helping at home far exceeded his efforts in classrooms. Paul, already known as Dr. No, continued to sink beneath his fear of anyone or anything new and cried most mornings when he was reminded he had to go to kindergarten. And Andrea developed a strange pattern. Every other time she would return from a visit with her mother, Andi would begin acting out, refusing to do habitual acts such as brushing her teeth or going to bed. Acting under my own stresses, I'd aggravate her further by pushing the issue, and soon enough I was shouting and she was crying in her room for the next half hour.

I kept a journal on Toni—missed appointments, unkept promises to the kids, statements, and acts made in front of them—in preparation for that courtroom showdown. The one I'll always remember was when Andi asked, "Dad, did you ever love Mom? She says you didn't."

I suppose the point at which we truly touched bottom was in a series of events surrounding court-ordered counseling. Our county had just joined many other legal jurisdictions in requiring counseling when there was a child custody dispute. My opinion of it, five years later, is that it was almost as one-sided and accusatory as our previous court encounters.

Certainly, I didn't provide an auspicious beginning to the session. It was the first time since the separation that I had had a chance to confront Toni face to face on matters I learned had been going on behind my back, including men she had seen and lies she had told me. The counselor, in my mind, immediately swept my righteous indignation out with the trash and began accusing me of blocking what was good for the children. Of course, that's the way I saw it as an outraged man, but it didn't help that Toni saw the counselor as an ally or that my attorney warned me of possible attempts by the counseling service to provide information that I was psychologically unfit to have custody.

Memo to the divorce court systems: This needs to be fixed.

Through the two sessions we had, the counselor came up with a shared custody plan that was so equally balanced it was like Solomon splitting that baby in two. It involved a complex trade-off every two days on a fourteen-day cycle, plus alternating holidays and split summer vacation times. I was so demoralized and confused I agreed to think about it.

By the next time we appeared in court in early 1994, I had thought about it, and I thought this plan was impossibly complex and totally unworkable. (We have enough problems with a much less complex joint parenting agreement, as it is.) When we stood in court, I was amazed to hear the counselor say I had agreed to her plan. "I do not," I said, and our hearing stopped right then.

The best thing about hitting bottom is that from there you have the chance to push off. Toni was obviously upset by the hearing, and my lawyer urged me to talk to her right then. In the muted sunlight of a large hallway outside the courtrooms, we sat down and talked about what we really wanted. I wanted a major role in raising my children. Toni wanted to get her life started again, and to do that she needed money to live on and money for college.

That was when the lawyers became negotiators, and we hammered out a settlement. It took a second mortgage to pay for some of it (along with the legal fees), but by August 31, 1994, the fifteenth anniversary of when I had asked her to marry me, the marriage was dissolved. Toni moved to a nearby town, and regular visitation began. We began to develop a partnership centered on raising and educating the kids, and my bitterness and anger began to fade.

But, even through the bitter times, joyous discoveries poked through like crocuses in the snow. I learned I could comfort a child's nightmare and that it could be a pleasure just sitting in the front car of a subway train riding up and riding back to no special destination. My social life became museums, hikes at the dunes, and Disney movies. I loved honking the car horn as I drove up the driveway at home, because I knew I'd hear a shout of "Daddy!" when I hit the door. Learning to double-knot shoelaces, to drill and correct on homework, that I could serve baked chicken only once a month and get them to eat it—all the bits and pieces of in-the-field parenting training were like merit badges to an Eagle Scout, battle ribbons to a veteran.

And one of the most important lessons of fatherhood came from this time. I learned that there is a blessing in the resilience of children. Anyone who cares about his or her child will worry about doing things wrong, about suddenly making that fatal error that destroys the child and the family. But things are not quite so crucial, though crucial they are. You can make honest mistakes, as long as you own up to them and try to correct them. Children will forget and forgive, out of love. And if you act out of love, can you truly fail?

These lessons and pleasures continued in regular progression as life seemed to settle down. Then I got a promotion at work to a position roughly equivalent to the one I had not gotten. It was a different challenge, but it didn't require the in-office time that the other job would have. I made a week-long trip for leadership training, and the household did not fall apart. I felt more and more like I could do this.

That feeling of confidence grew, even as the mistakes showed up and I had to learn new ways of doing things. I had no choice but to go back to the way my mother had raised me, but I tried to temper it with the love and masculine concern my stepfather had given me. I tried a few parenting books for fathers, but reading time was still at a premium, and much of what I read didn't seem to apply to me and my family.

My next step was possibly the most foolhardy, even though I think it has ended successfully. I had always wanted a graduate degree and had even promised my mother I would go back for one. A former supervisor of mine had gotten his master's in management through an executive master's program, and that looked most like what I wanted to do. In the summer of 1996 I applied for admission to the executive program at the Kellogg Graduate School of Management at Northwestern University, a top-ranked program at one of the five best business schools in America. I also laid the groundwork with my bosses at the *Tribune*.

When I got the letter from Kellogg, I convinced myself that I had been turned down. When I opened it and read, "Congratulations . . . ," I immediately put the letter on my desk and wandered the house. It took several minutes to calm down enough to read the rest of the letter. And then Mother *Tribune* came through for me again, paying the considerable tuition up front and requiring me to reimburse the company for only 10 percent of the cost.

The Kellogg program is nothing if not rigorous—two full-week sessions, one in each of the two years, and the rest of the time filled with all-day classes on alternating Fridays and Saturdays. Study-group meetings, reading, and report writing filled from ten to twenty hours a week, and I found I had to create a new work-parent-sleep system. I tried to get shopping done in the time window between kids off to school and time for work. I dropped my gym membership since I was headed straight from work to home, where dinner and chores and kids' homework awaited me. I found I could not do my homework with them—they had too many questions, and I couldn't combine Porter's "Five Forces" and Andi's ten geography questions in my mind. Therefore, after dinner I concentrated on getting them prepared for the next day's schooling and getting them to bed, and I went to bed at the same time.

But for the next two years my alarm went off sometime between 4:00 and 5:00 A.M. so that I could finish my reading or write that report for the weekend's class.

It was difficult and exhilarating. I was in class with execs who had years of experience and better business training than dumb-journalist me. I felt I did well, and I must say that one of the greatest pleasures was hearing one person or another at work or at school say, "I don't know how you do it." It made me feel gutsy, like I was more than meeting a challenge, I was surpassing what was expected and succeeding in a quest.

How much a detriment grad school was to the kids, I still don't know. We had less time for trips and movies out, and that may have allowed the video-game monster to put a stranglehold on my two boys. Andi became a neighborhood gossip and gadfly, visiting kids up and down the block and joining a recycle club and improvisational dance class. Paul is becoming more accepting of the necessity, and open to the possible pleasure, of school and learning. Meanwhile, Michael is still dependent on the grace of God and a fast outfield to keep his grades above failure.

I graduated from Kellogg with a master's in management in December 1997, just when the work on this book reached high gear. I have continued my work with my kids' schools and have learned to respect many of the teachers my children have. Our household of one adult, three kids, and a dog has expanded to include four pet mice. My finances have rebounded (thanks, Mother *Trib*), and I am now considering a major remodeling of my house, with the end result to be that we sell it and move. I have even read some books not on a course syllabus, as well as two newspapers most days.

But I look at Nick's testimony in Chapter 4, and I realize that there is something missing here—time for the nonwork, nondad me. I've started dating occasionally, but I fear I talk too much about being a dad. I still see movies on my own, and most of my friends are at the end of a phone line or contacted by modem. I rejoined the gym but still haven't gone in. I think I need to try for some other renewable pleasures.

One of the things I miss most is the support of a true in-house partner. Friends and family are fine, but someone to share the fears with and plot the plans with and share the fun with, someone to trust, adult to adult, is not replaceable by friendship. I refuse to "mommy-shop," because I don't feel it's fair to the potential mommy, but finding a partner in this life would not be unwelcome.

In the meantime, there is that exaltation. Every summer I graduate (again) from three school grades. Every so often, a panting buck bursts from the woods of Indiana Dunes State Park and stands in front of our car. I can still get group hugs and quick tickles and a "pile-up" of kid-and-Dad bodies on my bed. Michael will cook dinner; Andi will write a great, funny story; Paul will gloat over an improving math score. And I am plotting my invasion of the video-game fortress, if only to rescue them from the empty glitter of special effects. There are always things to do, a higher purpose to espouse, a more challenging task to accomplish.

For me, to father is always a joy.

Part III

Taking Care
of Yourself

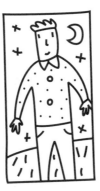

WHAT A PIECE of work is man: strong, quiet, uncomplaining. Emotional only when that bonehead referee makes a bad call, especially against your homegrown athlete. And you take that self-contained aura of quiet confidence and unexpressed emotion into every saloon, office, and parent-teacher conference you encounter. Straight to the grave.

Since you are a good dad, the last thing you think of is yourself, right? Oh, so wrong. As one single mom author we know explained it, "How can you have anything for your children if you don't have something inside yourself to give?"

This is an era of pop psychology and continuous counseling, but that doesn't mean you should ignore your own wellbeing to buck the trend. Help may well be out there, and you should feel no shame in seeking it.

Just as we said earlier in our chapter on help with the kids, help for yourself is something you usually need, may want, and shouldn't hesitate to get. Ask yourself this: Who is stronger, the healthy man who sought assistance to bring back his power or the ill man who wouldn't take the time to seek a cure?

Help comes in many forms—counseling and psychiatric services, support groups, family and friends, and individual relationships. It also comes from sources as varied as employee assistance plans, private insurance, public health programs, and the Internet. (We personally would not include any psychic phone friends, but, hey, a man's gotta do what a man's gotta do.) Some help comes at a cost, and perhaps one as high as damaging your career and your future. But much of it can be found inexpensively or at no cost. The main thing you have to do is ask for it.

More than most, this section is written for the single father. Not that all of us don't need our heads shrunk a bit on occasion, but the issues of counseling, stress relief, and dating, when focused on the man alone with children, have specific answers that don't apply elsewhere.

Our next chapter deals with those sources of aid for a troubled solo dad, from a head massage to a good workout to an evening out. And the final chapter delves into the greatest untapped resource for assistance that we have—fathers themselves.

Last Things First: Your Emotional Health

WE SAY IT OFTEN, but what is still an extremely important thing for us to remember—something we need to communicate to everybody else—is that you have to make time for yourself. If you're not making time for yourself, you're not doing as well as you think you are.

You may feel you are spending important time with the kids, but you may be spending it in a poor fashion. You may be spending it riding on them; you may be spending it yelling and screaming. You may not be spending it in a time when you feel relaxed and can share with them and accept them as just children. You have to have the time to get your own head together.

However, just as with the challenges of dealing with your children, dealing with your head problems is not something you have to do alone. Numerous counseling, support group, and mental health services are available. Some may require big bucks, others big commitment. But all require you to realize the need and be willing to do something to fill the need.

RD: The need was and still is a lack of control in my own life, not being able to decide how I should view my married life, what to do with it. I can say on a logical level that it was probably a marriage that was doomed from the start. I can say on a logical level that it created three great kids, so you can't say too much bad about it. But you know that whenever someone says, "I don't want you anymore," it has a tremendous, tremendous negative impact on your emotions, your ego, and everything. So having to deal with that was too much to do by myself.

I went into counseling not too long after the marital separation began, and I saw a counselor for a while. There were occasions when she actually made suggestions. They were expressed as "I can't be you, but were I in this situation, I might. . . ." But it also included the typical on-the-couch analysis, with lots of questions like "Do you think it could be from your father?"

Then she tried to switch me to group therapy, and I didn't feel comfortable at all in group. I went one time and then stopped showing up. By the time I thought of going back, the company health insurance, which was paying for this, changed and they contracted with an employee assistance program, so I couldn't go back anyway. But I remember calling her and—believe it or not—she put a guilt trip on me. She said, "You know, all those people in the group were expecting you to come back, and you didn't. You let the group down." Thanks a lot.

When I felt like I needed to talk to somebody else, I went through the employee assistance program. The program's counselor used a more modern, quick, "Let's show you how you can feel good" approach. The counseling did not seek out the root cause of problems. It's being paid for by bosses who want you to get well enough to be functional at work. The counselor's techniques included sitting down at the end of the day and writing down what you had felt during that day. There was a written questionnaire, and you wrote what made you feel good, what made you feel bad, what good things you did for yourself and others, what might make you feel better. There was a specific number of items that needed to be written down, especially in the "feel good" categories. The main idea, I guess, was to get you out of concentrating on the negative and into realizing that there is happiness in every day and more good than bad when you really look at it. It may sound like *Pollyanna*, but it worked pretty well. The only problem was finding the time to sit down and write. But after practicing the written task several times, I could do the exercise mentally, just taking a few minutes to assess my day and find the good that had happened and that I had done. It helped a lot.

Anyway, how about you, Nick? I know you have talked about depression. When did that come up? I know there is a time we have never talked much about, when your youngest son, Stephen, was struck and killed just after he left the school bus.

NB: Yeah, in 1985. That's when Stephen died, and with everything else going on, it was really tough. In fact, the navy was beginning to get a little short with me, wondering, "When are you going to get your ass back to work?"

RD: How long were you out?

NB: I took almost a month of emergency leave there. I felt that things had to be done, and I kind of ran on autopilot, almost glad that these things had to be done even though they seemed somewhat bothersome. I was taking care of the funeral arrangements, notifying people, getting the kids off to school and such.

RD: Didn't this happen at the end of the school year?

NB: There were about two days of school left. But you still have to deal with all these things: you have to deal with the kids; you have to get supper on. And after about a week, when we finally got all the family out there, having some of my family around helped and I was trying to play the good host but just being really active. It was kind of like a high.

Then everybody left, and we were left with this as the way things are. We have one less person in the family. How do you deal with it now? Patty and I just didn't talk. We were so out of phase on that. I didn't want to talk and she did, and I'm very stubborn. And then it got around finally to where I wanted to talk and she didn't, and that's how it went for us.

RD: Did it get into you taking blame for the accident?

NB: I took some blame for the accident. I was in the house sleeping, as I was going on mid-watches. I did not go out to meet his bus. When I got out there and saw what had happened, I ran over and I was holding his hand until the paramedics got there, trying to talk to him.

Now Karl, when he was a year old, had tried to come downstairs by sliding on the rail, except he fell, bounced off the rail, and then fell on the hardwood floor. That scared the bejesus out of us. We got an ambulance and took him to the hospital. Patty spent the night in the hospital with him, and I had Nick at home. The next day I went into the hospital asking, "God, is he going to live?" Because he had just lain there and moaned a low moan and didn't move. I mean, talk about fear. So the next morning I got into the hospital, and the staff had had to put a net over the top of the crib, because Karl was trying to crawl out and was jumping like nothing had happened.

And Stephen was lying there like Karl had, but I was holding his hand, and I could feel how incredibly frightened this little boy was. I just held on to him for as long as I could until the paramedics got there, and I've always regretted that when they arrived I moved out of the way. And I've always felt that if I had just stayed with him and held on to him, things might have been different.

So I had that to deal with, and I still deal with it. And afterward, I just hit a period where I really didn't care. I got into group therapy. Actually I wasn't looking for a group; I just wanted to talk to somebody. I went to the navy doctor, put some things on a questionnaire. "Have you ever thought about suicide?" I said, "Sure, what the heck." Well, that got someone's attention, which was what I wanted to do. I really thought, "Yes, I have. I have thought about suicide sometimes, but then I think this is the last big hurrah. This is the last big cheat, suicide. Once you've done it, you can't undo it, and then you find out, 'Hey, I didn't want to do this!' and now you're stuck." But as long as you're alive, you've got a chance to do something or change something.

So I was in group for a while, and that helped. I was diagnosed with depression; that was the medical diagnosis. Later on, I think about a year or two later, I was going to the Veterans Administration medical center. I actually wanted to go to find out about a hearing problem, and you have to go through this whole gamut of tests. The doctor said, "Yeah, you're getting along, but you're still having a problem with depression." It was not something that he felt that there was any need to prescribe medication for, so he said, "Knowing that you have it, you can probably deal with it and maybe set up some counseling." But not long after that I got the other job in Madison, Indiana, and I moved, so I never really looked into it.

In Indiana, I was fairly busy and I did make a couple of friends, so I had quite a bit to do, and then the kids came down.

RD: Keeping "fairly busy" is men's therapy.

NB: It keeps you from thinking about needing therapy.

RD: *That* I have learned far too well. Keep busy, then I don't have to think about it. If I were still in grad school, then I wouldn't be able to think as much about Michael's problems with schoolwork, my own social life, anything that is stressing me now.

What "other ways" do you use to handle stress?

NB: Well, you need to have people to talk to, and you really need more than one, if for no other reason than you can say the same story to two or three people and it's new each time, but if you start calling the same person and going through the same diatribe, it gets boring.

And exercise. I noticed that over the last five or six years I've been slowly gaining weight. I kept thinking that I had to get it off, but as long as I was in the reserves, twice a year I had to get into an exercise program to pass the physical readiness test. Well, as of August of 1996, I've retired from the reserves. I don't have to do that anymore, and I have gained about twenty pounds. There's a big difference, because I had a big change in my activity level. So now I am modifying my diet and getting back into some exercise.

RD: I've never had an exercise program that lasted for years, but I've had a number of times when I've started and stopped. The good ones I started and stayed with for several months.

I was gaining weight throughout my marriage, as men do. As the kids came, I felt like I needed to get home earlier, so I'd come straight home and not go to a gym to work out. I have exercise equipment at home, but I go through long periods when I don't touch it.

When I was in the master's program, there just was no time. Now that I've graduated, I'm using writing the book as an excuse—I'm saying, "You just don't have time to get up and exercise. You've got to get the book done."

I actually have rejoined the health club after not being a member for three years. I rejoined specifically thinking, "Well, I can get a very inexpensive, two-day-a-week membership, and I can use Friday or Saturday as one day, and then I'll just have to find a way of sneaking in another one. Maybe I'll do both a Friday and a Saturday, when the kids are with Mom." But I haven't gone at all yet.

NB: I believe that there is a very strong relationship between physical and mental and emotional health.

RD: What kind of exercise program do you generally follow?

NB: Last year I did virtually nothing. That's what caused all the problems. What I started doing is, I pulled out my skier machine and set it up down in the basement, and I've got some weights down there. What I have found that I am comfortable with doing is to go down there and do some stretching to warm up. Then I do about ten minutes of weightlifting and then twenty minutes on the skier, and after that I'll do another five or ten minutes of light calisthenics. If I can put aside forty-five minutes, then I can get in a decent amount of exercise.

RD: My routine almost always involves a lot of weightlifting. What I do now, when I do get up in the morning, is abdominal exercises as my warmup, and I try for an aerobic burn by doing them without resting between exercises. I'll do between four and six sets of abdominal exercises, and then, depending on what time I have, I'll do a weight circuit with dumbbells, concentrating on my arms, chest, and back. That's up to six exercises done slowly and, again, without rest. I try to do twelve to fifteen repetitions of each exercise. That is also an aerobic as well as strength-building circuit, but it won't build big muscles. Or I'll just do pushups in three variations—close-grip, wide, and regular, maybe fifteen of each, if I can.

My real aerobic workout, when the weather is nice, is to go out and do in-line skating. I've tried running; running hurts my knees. I've tried biking, and I can't sit on that bike seat. But skating really relaxes me. I lose the ability to think about anything except skating. I can't think about problems. All I can think about is getting around the next corner and avoiding the next patch of bad asphalt. I try not to stay away from the house for more than forty-five minutes, and I don't know if the kids miss me for that forty-five minutes, but I really need that time. My morning exercises will take about forty-five minutes, and I try to do them on alternate days. I strive for at least three days of exercise a week.

NB: I try to go for three to five days a week. Also, from forty-five minutes to an hour is what I'm looking for. If you do less than that, it's not very effective.

There's something else that I've tried to do, but I've just let myself get totally away from it: I've taken classes in tai chi. I went with Karl, and it was very interesting.

RD: That's something all the kids and I could do together, and we need more of that. We just went bowling for the first time in a long while, and we need to do more exercise together.

NB: I think it's really important, especially for single parents, to put that exercise time aside. Sometimes it will have to slide, but you really have to make that effort to put it in, because it's keeping you together in more ways than just physically, and you're better able to handle the other problems that come up then.

RD: I was just reading an essay in a fitness magazine that talked about the "I don't have enough time" excuse for not exercising. Interestingly enough, the author did not say that it was the argument of the lazy. He said people sincerely want to work out, but they don't know how to find time, and he gave several suggestions, including cutting down on idle TV and telephone time, eating healthily to prevent diet problems from destroying your workout's positive effects, and making a workout a high priority. Sounds good to me.

Let's move into an even more personal area: from not making time for yourself to not making time for yourself and another person.

RD: This I think is one of the biggest, most glaring differences between you and me. You are able to acknowledge that you need to have somebody else in your life, some other adult, and I find it very hard to do. I find it very hard to enjoy myself when I'm out. On a date I find it very hard to say in my own mind that this person wants to spend time with me. And I can be thinking that I should be spending time somewhere else because it's only "my time" and not time for the family.

I go to lunch with people at work, or I meet people after, many of them very attractive, but I feel I have no right to their time because so much of my time is shared with the kids. I don't meet very many women with kids. Of course, I'm the one who avoids places like Parents Without Partners because I don't want a "mommy shop." So how am I going to meet people to date?

I have just recently gotten involved in a fathers' support group, and that has been one of the few things that I do for myself that I really value. I really appreciate being able to talk to them, to listen to them and hear what they have gone through and what they're going through now and to share ideas. But I want you to talk about your social life.

NB: I started losing the social life before I was divorced, when we were dealing with my wife's illness. Once I got divorced, though, I had some hesitation about social life. Sure, I wanted to date, but what was I going to go after?

RD: Did you feel like damaged goods or like you were coming with extra baggage?

NB: Yeah, I felt like I was in a very weak position as far as any social interaction with someone else. But I needed to know what I was ready to give up to somebody and what I wanted from somebody. It made for a difficult time, plus I needed to take care of the kids, too. I also needed to see to my career, and my time got eaten up. So I really didn't go out much at all when I first got divorced.

RD: It takes you a while just to get over the fact that you are divorced.

NB: Actually, that is one of problems I had all along. I didn't really understand what I was dealing with, with the divorce and what I had to go through. Looking back, I wish someone had told me about what was happening to me. You have a failed marriage; placing blame isn't going to help. What are you dealing with, and how do you deal with it?

RD: Having a failed marriage doesn't mean that you are a failure.

NB: That's right.

RD: That's something that took me a while to accept, and I still find myself going back to saying, "Well, it was your fault."

NB: Yeah, there are a lot of questions like "Could I have done something different to save it? Where's the blame? Where's the guilt coming from? I'm going to have it poured all over me. I'm going to wallow in it." I did that, too.

Where I worked, I did meet someone to go out with, and we had fun a few times, but it was kind of awkward. There weren't too many other people at work for me to meet. It was hard for me to meet people. It was a small community, a close community.

With the kids around, it was easier to say, "I don't have time for it," and you can put it off. When they get a little bit older and they want to go do something with their friends, you realize that you are on your own. You have to deal with it then.

RD: Someone once told me of the personal philosophy of a divorced woman she knew. The divorced woman allegedly said, "Let him have the kids. I'm not going to be old and sitting in a corner forgotten and alone when they grow up and go off and have their own lives. I'm going to have some fun now so that it will be with me when I get old."

It sounds harsh and cold, and I'm sure the person telling the story put it in the coldest fashion that she could. But for me, having fun before I get old is not high on my agenda. I don't worry about being seventy years old and alone. I figure I'll find something to do with myself.

But probably I should worry about that. To hear you talk about the difficulty of finding somebody and that need to find somebody as the kids go off and have their own social life and find other things to do, finding yourself without somebody to share things with, makes me frightened. I think I'm in denial about loneliness, saying, "That won't be me. That won't be me."

I've got only a few years. Paul turned ten in June. That means in less than six years he's going to have his own social life, and all the rest of them are going to be doing the same. And I do get lonely. I do wonder about what I am going to do. I go to a movie by myself, and I don't even have anybody to talk to about it.

I have a few friends left from college and after college, and I suppose there will be times when we can renew some of the friendships, but they have families, and we all know how families can pull you away from a lot of your old buddy-buddy friendships.

NB: Yeah, well, part of finding somebody is realizing what you want to find. Part of realizing that is dealing with where you are in your divorce and how you have dealt with it. I ran into another group out here that I wish I had found years ago. It's a program called Together We Can Make It. It was an eight-week course, it met once a week, and you had to be divorced or separated and getting a divorce. At the second meeting you had to make a decision of whether you were going to finish the course.

It was a fairly structured environment. We had about six people in our group. However, it's a group that has a lot of things in common. We all had varied backgrounds, but as far as the divorce situations we were dealing with, we were all fairly close in what we had to deal with.

There was a book with material to read about what you were doing in the sessions, and there were exercises at the end of each chapter that you were supposed to do between classes. I found that

I could think about these things I was feeling and going through, but it's not the same as actually writing it down. I was traveling for work, and I had to miss one of the group meetings now and again. But while I was on the plane, I had my laptop computer with me, and I would just do the exercises, do the readings. And I found that this was really helpful to me. It helped me to better understand what I had gone through. I was better able to understand the need to have social contact and not just friends. A friend you can call and talk to, and build a relationship with on several levels.

So, that being said, I've been able to know what am I looking for, what kind of relationship I want and how soon I want it. I know that I don't want to rush into something, and I've learned more about the relationship that I was in that ended, so I can avoid doing it all over again.

You need to understand what needs you have, what you are doing, and look for some relationship complementary to that. I don't know if I could put up with someone exactly like me, and it would probably get rather boring. I don't want someone who is simply going to agree with me all the time. You need a little bit of conflict. I tend to shy away from somebody who is willing to do anything just to be with me.

RD: For me, that's scary.

NB: Yeah, it is scary. I see that as becoming a dictatorial relationship. You've got one person who is totally in power, the other one is totally submissive, and one scary thought is: What if I'm not around at a crucial time? Is this other person going to be able to jump in and take care of things? I'm very reluctant to believe that someone willing to be totally submissive will do that. She may be capable of it, but being capable and being willing to do it may not go hand in hand.

I believe the key to answering these issues is in my relationship with my current girlfriend. As much as I desire a permanent relationship with another woman, I find that I am not as prepared to make a permanent commitment as I thought I was. I have very deep feelings for my girlfriend, but we have some important issues to resolve: How do you merge families? How do you avoid trapping the older child into being a convenient, unpaid baby-sitter for the younger children of the other individual? How do you handle discipline? How do you decide where to live and how mingled your finances should be? What level of authority is granted to each of the adults, and what responsibilities are expected toward the other's children?

Being involved with a single-parent support group like Parents Without Partners has been quite a blessing. I have had the opportunity to discuss single-parent issues with others in the same boat. Just finding out that there are other single parents, especially fathers who are custodial parents, has been a major relief. I have also joined another group designed for singles, the Friends of Mercy, and met other people. I have been fortunate to get involved in these groups. They have not solved all my parenting problems, but they have increased the probability of solving them, or at least handling them to a better degree.

I still have quite a bit of work to do to deal with being a solo dad, but I believe I am making pretty good progress.

Fathers of the World, Unite!

So, BY NOW you should know the truth: if you are male and on any occasion watch over children, you are a solo dad. Because being a solo dad doesn't just mean being a single father; it includes all men trying to father kids alone, from those who may be solo for an afternoon to those who may be solo for as long as the kids are kids. Yes, there are part-time solo dads and occasional solo dads, some very limited ones, and sometimes even those who are volunteers.

And, since we are all in this together, it is high time we got together and recognized it. Fathers today have a lot to learn, and other fathers have a lot to teach them. What we know is different from what mothers know, but it is no less valid knowledge in the ways of rearing a child. We need to hear it, we need to share it, and we need to affirm that it is true.

There is nothing that says men can't discuss Junior's coping skills or Sally's math anxiety along with the ball scores and the work wars as we meet over a beer. But something keeps us from it. Psychiatrists say, "Men don't follow up." There are few fathers' support groups, and most of those that do exist are directed toward special situations like the impoverished or unwed teens. Even the World Wide Web appears nearly vacant of areas where fathers swap dad stories of triumph and concern.

Maybe it's our macho posturing, our fear of showing "our feminine side." But raising kids ain't picking petunias. There are male ways of nurturing, supporting, and loving children, and those children need the masculine touch as much as the feminine one.

We want to turn this last chapter into our manifesto, our call to arms. Each of us will express what we want fathers—single and married, foster and adopted, temporary and permanent—to know about themselves and each other. We want to call all of you to join in celebrating fathering and honoring fatherhood.

And we are also holding out our hands to the millions of solo dads everywhere. We want to make contact with you and keep you informed. Therefore, we have an e-mail address, solodads@aol.com, where we would like to address your concerns and answer your questions. If there is enough interest, maybe we can establish a bulletin board or a full-fledged Web page. But whatever the result, we want to hear from you.

Our manifesto follows, but never forget this: we need each other as fathers and as friends.

NB: If I can try to encapsulate what I would like to get across with this book, it would have to be the following:

- Men should not feel that they are unable to be good single parents. Our society has told men that they are not nurturing parents, that they are somehow unable to adapt to the sudden needs of single parenthood. Parenthood is a daunting challenge, especially on your own, so it is no wonder that some would opt out. But it is not the end of the world or even of life as we know it. Don't be afraid of being a parent. The challenges are unique and constantly changing, but they are not insurmountable.

- Don't be afraid to ask for help. No one can be a parent all the time and get everything done that needs to be done. It is all right to ask for help. Look around for groups for single dads. A group for single parents should include single dads. This gives you somewhere to go to meet people who have a situation similar to your own. And there are quite a few single dads out there. Let's talk to each other, if for no other reason than to validate our own situations and feelings.

- Surprise—men have feelings, too. We do not display them in the same manner or act strictly on the basis of feelings, but we have them. By getting to know other single dads, we can have a way to vent them safely and keep them from building up and coming out inappropriately or even violently.

- Before you become a father, think about it. I have a very low opinion of men who become fathers and really don't want to and don't care and then take off. I can understand why they might have children—because they are too ignorant to understand birth control or too arrogant to use it. Before you become a father, consider what kind of father you want to be. Don't let someone talk you into the stereotype that dads can't cook or do laundry. Men are quite capable of nurturing. In fact, we are every bit as capable as women, and we should be allowing ourselves to take these duties on.

- I've seen more dads who are willing to fight for custody, and I think they should really think about this. If you are going through a divorce, get it over with. Don't horse around. Then take care of the kids. Don't be afraid to go for custody; maybe Mom isn't going to be a very good mom.

- Really think hard about the values that you are teaching your kids. And you don't teach by sitting them down and saying, "This is a positive value; this is a negative value." The way you act, the way you lead your life, the way you take responsibility, and how you approach your responsibilities teach the lessons in the best way.

- Concentrate on being the best dad you can, regardless. Don't worry about the other parent. Don't waste time running down the other parent; that's "ex" bashing. It's not worth it, and most of the time it backfires on you anyway. Be positive, and don't be afraid to be the dad.

There are more single dads every day. We are capable of child rearing, and we should not be afraid to admit that we can nurture our children. We have a lot to offer our children, so let's not deny ourselves to them. After all, it is through our children that we achieve our own sense of immortality.

RD: I am a dad watcher; I admit it. I watch them pull wagonloads of squealing kids safely across the street. I watch them carry babies out of airports. I watch them in the parks, teaching their sons and daughters how not to "throw like a girl." I watch them discipline and touch and frown and hug.

I watch because I am proud of them, proud of all of us who have found that duty and happiness combine, not in procreation but in bringing up those we procreated. I watch them to applaud and compare and learn.

I often feel very inadequate at this fathering thing, at a loss and doing the wrong thing or not knowing the right one. Like many men of my generation, I got little instruction in being a father from my own father or his father. So I look at fathers in life, in books, and in film to try to be a better father. Some lessons aren't easy to learn.

But the greatest resource for any father is other fathers, and I find that resource as scattered and hard to read as a great city library where all of the books are on the floor. A waste of space, a waste of knowledge, and a waste of support.

That support is sorely needed among us men. Despite years of change, it is still nearly impossible for a man to gain full custody of his children, even when he is obviously the more responsible parent, and while joint parenting has become more available, its imposition can make illogical demands on all the family members involved.

The "tender years" philosophy is just part of the legal justification. Men are denied access to their children for all kinds of reasons—accusations, some unprovable, of sexual assault and abuse; prejudice against unwed fathers; suspicions of the motives of men who would nurture children; the alleged male reputation for physical violence. Meanwhile, father-first campaigns would have us reject the societal gains wrought by the women's rights movement in favor of eighteenth-century male domination. They undercut our rightful claims with women who would not be subjugated again.

The fractured status of the American family and the new methods of technology-assisted birth make our standing in the preparation of the next generation dubious at best. We are in Huxley's *Brave New World*, pleasure machines without purpose, without fathers, and without progeny. And when we stand, we stand alone, one man here and one man there. Being a father is the most important role we can ever have in our lives, but we can't join together to teach and learn our roles. We rely, instead, on individual effort and trial and error.

Even the educational processes we have set up can be seen as working against our own good. Admittedly, it is thoroughly understandable that public schools teach child care with mechanical babies that are programmed for tears or sacks of flour to weigh down a teenager's rush toward adulthood. Society benefits when teens are made to believe that they should never have children before they are mature enough to provide for them. But in young men's ears, this message can be added to the street-corner talk about not taking responsibility for the results of unprotected sex. When do we teach boys to want children and want to take care of them?

I support all of Nick's points, and they represent the issues discussed throughout this book. But I want to emphasize one point here: No book can teach you all you need to know to be a good father, just as no one man can be a good father to all children. We need lessons learned again and again. We need new methods and lots of variations. We need practical advice and expert testimony.

We cannot get everything we need from books, TV shows, or listen-in-the-car audiotapes. We can get it only from each other, from fathers past and fathers future. It is time we took our thoughts beyond our reptilian brains and pooled our resources for our children's good.

Let us talk together, one on one or in groups, on the Internet or on the phone, in schools and in support groups. Let us relate our experiences and listen to the experiences of others—including the experiences of women raising children. Let us learn skills that add to our natural instincts to make a family and help it grow.

As Nick said, it is through our children that we achieve our own sense of immortality. Raising our children well is our way of making that immortality possible, because raising our children poorly endangers our world and all that thousands of generations of human life have striven to put here.

Just as Nick and I did to put this book together, we can talk, we can share, we can learn. It's all for our own good and for our continued survival.